RICHMOND'S
MAIN STREET

STORIES FROM THE WALL STREET OF THE SOUTH

RICHMOND'S MAIN STREET

STORIES FROM THE WALL STREET OF THE SOUTH

John B. Keefe, Sr.

2018

RICHMOND

MainStreetRichmondBook@gmail.com

Publisher: Wayne Dementi
Dementi Milestone Publishing, Inc.
Manakin-Sabot, Virginia 23103

www.DementiMilestonePublishing.com

The author and Dementi Milestone Publishing, Inc., disclaim all liability in connection with the use of this book.

ISBN 978-0-9777220-7-5

Library of Congress Control Number 2018903609

Front cover painting: "The Corner," painting by William P. Schubmehl

Back cover: New York Stock Exchange, Library of Congress;
9th & Main signs, John B. Keefe

CONTENTS

THE INTERVIEWS

☞

APPENDICES

FOREWORD

Go to almost any town or city in the United States and you will find a Main Street. In the majority of small towns it has been the major route running through the heart of the community.

That was true in my hometown in Tennessee. Like most Main Streets in small town America, our Main Street represented the economic and power center of the community when I was growing up in the 1950s. Today, however, that Main Street is a mere shadow of itself. Empty storefronts and abandoned lots now mark the once-vibrant thoroughfare.

With more and more people abandoning rural and small-town America for big cities, broad swaths of the country have been emptying out, with most moving to urban areas like Richmond.

Main Street in Richmond is another matter. In many respects this important corridor of business and commerce has served as a metaphor for the entire city itself.

Beginning in the late eighteenth century, Main Street was the site of a thriving market at East Main Street near Shockoe Creek. By the mid-nineteenth century, the market included nearly twenty slave auction houses, as Virginia became the largest exporter of slaves to the Deep South. The slave trade created enormous wealth for some individuals, much of which was destroyed during the Civil War.

The great Evacuation Fire of 1865, started when retreating Confederate forces surrendered the city to a conquering Union army, left Richmond devastated for years. But by the turn of the twentieth century, the city's fortunes turned for the better, driven to a significant extent by a thriving tobacco products manufacturing base. Until the late 1960s, Main Street, like the downtown as a whole, was home to a flourishing business community, replete with retail stores, restaurants, law offices, and numerous other commercial enterprises.

It also developed into a leading financial center, home to thriving investment firms, large banks, and since 1914, the Federal Reserve Bank for the Fifth District. By the 1980s, Richmond had more stock exchange members than any other city in the South. Local names such as Branch,

Scott, Wheat, and Davenport were well known in financial circles far beyond the confines of Richmond.

The next three decades were not so kind to Main Street and downtown Richmond. Local banks that had been major power brokers for decades were bought out by larger banks in other cities. Some of the businesses that had been long anchored to downtown began to flee to the so-called edge city of Innsbrook in the far west end of Henrico County. The leading downtown department stores, Thalhimers and Miller & Rhoads, went out of business in the 1990s. And with the rise of Short Pump as a major retail center west of Innsbrook, it seemed that downtown Richmond was doomed to further decline. Home to a dozen or so Fortune 500 companies in the 1980s, little by little Richmond saw them move their headquarters elsewhere or merge with other companies located in other cities.

Through all of these dramatic changes, Main Street has not only survived, it has in many ways thrived. John Keefe has spent many hours interviewing dozens of people with knowledge of the story of this vital investment community. This is an important oral history of a southern city that will be appreciated by general public readers and scholars alike.

I salute John for taking on this task to help all of us understand just what makes Richmond tick.

Charles F. Bryan, Jr., Ph.D.
President and CEO emeritus
Virginia Historical Society

THANKS

I am deeply grateful for the participation of each and every interviewee. The meetings consumed a lot of their time, including follow-up reviews and edits. I suspected I was on to something from the first one. By the last one, I knew the quality and relevance of their personal recollections would overcome my limited oral historian skills.

Special thanks to Robert Keefe for his advice and many long hours in assembling *Main Street's* text and photo layout.

I'm in debt to Louis Bowman, whose insights, judgment, and introductions were especially helpful. Mike Mendelson's advice and edits were invaluable. I appreciate the late hours and devotion to accuracy of Pam Deyerle and Steven Deyerle, transcriptionists and copy editors at The Perfect Word. Bernice Lipson Katz, Pat Branch, Carlisle Branch, Linda Ludeke, Kendall Avery, Tom Keefe, and Peter Keefe assisted in various ways and made this book the better for it.

Ruth Erb, owner of the aptly named Book People independent book store, was generous with her advice. I thank the Virginia Historical Society and Anne Hobson Freeman for allowing me to excerpt Mrs. Freeman's interview with Carlyle Tiller.

David Kilman of the Richmond Public Library, Meghan Townes and Dana Puga of the Library of Virginia, and Nicole Kappatos of the Richmond Times-Dispatch helped a rookie author figure out how to locate much of the background and photographic material in this book.

A salute to the late Jim White, one of the great personalities of Main Street. I'd love to know what he's thinking about all this right now.

And love to Theresa, Rob, and John.

John B. Keefe
Richmond

PREFACE

The pause between his second and third words was probably no more than a beat, maybe two, but you were almost staring at your shoes before it was over. J. Harvie Wilkinson, Jr., former chairman of United Virginia Bankshares and former Media General director, rose to his feet. He was speaking in support of incumbent directors at Media General's annual shareholder meeting in 1988.

"Ladies . . . gentlemen . . . *Sugarman*." It was clear to the packed audience in the Virginia Museum of Fine Arts auditorium how Mr. Wilkinson felt about Hollywood TV producer Burt Sugarman and his hostile takeover attempt of the parent of Richmond's two daily newspapers.

And why wouldn't he feel that way? Wilkinson, and the Bryan family who controlled Media General, represented the Richmond way of doing things: steady, proper, long term. To many, Sugarman represented the Los Angeles way of doing things: flashy, crude, short term. One side was the custodian of a local institution of immense public trust. The other side produced *The Gong Show, The Dating Game*, and *The Newlywed Game*.

The home team crowd agreed with Mr. Wilkinson. He was met with applause when he finished. When Mr. Sugarman presented his case . . . polite golf claps. A few months later, Mr. Sugarman folded his tent. He sold his Media General stock back to the company for $100 million, a loss of $11 million. The $100 million sale price included $44 million in cash and a recycled newsprint mill valued at $56 million. His timing was good, or lucky; a year later he flipped the mill for $95 million.[1] The buyer's crystal ball could not have predicted that by 2007 the curtain would drop for good on that analog-age mill.

It was around this time that I thought of keeping notes, some kind of written trail, about the people I worked with in the stock market business in Richmond. I knew someday I'd want an accurate remembrance of the era. Of course, I never followed through, and my power of memory is not what it used to be. So, what to do? A couple of years ago I decided to create an oral history of the time. That way, I could let others do the hard work of remembering things. But I procrastinated on that idea, also.

What moved me to action was the death of my friend and former partner in institutional sales, Jim White, in late July 2017. Although I hadn't spoken to him in a while, I'd always assumed he'd be a big part of the project. I will no longer make assumptions like that.

Main Street is about the people who worked in Richmond's Main Street investment community (with some New York and Baltimore in the mix) in the 1980s and 1990s, a period of remarkable personalities and extraordinary change. Some of our storytellers began their careers in the 1950s, others in the 1990s. Some are retired, or left the business; many continue to run companies, provide investment counsel, and manage money for retirement systems, universities, shareholders and policyholders, institutions, and affluent individuals. They played a role in the greatest financial ride of our lifetimes.

❧

Just as Richmond counted itself a regional retailing center for much of the twentieth century, home to leading mercantile operations,[2] it was a major financial center, home to important banks and investment firms. In the 1970s, Richmond headquartered more New York Stock Exchange (NYSE) member firms—Abbott, Proctor & Paine; Anderson & Strudwick; Branch & Company; Branch, Cabell; Davenport; Scott & Stringfellow; and Wheat—than any city in the nation outside New York City. Ultimately, waves of financial services merger and acquisition activity, heavy regulatory burdens, and increasing technology requirements convinced all but Davenport to yield to larger, out-of-state partners.

That Richmond's biggest local firms were NYSE members was a point of pride. But they, and a few smaller firms, also belonged to the old Richmond Stock Exchange, one of twenty-four stock markets registered with the Securities and Exchange Commission in the 1930s.[3] Members met at noon daily in the First & Merchants Bank building on Ninth and Main Streets. The Exchange's purpose was to disseminate quotes and facilitate trading in local stocks, recalls the wonderful Bernice Lipson Katz, the RSE's secretary-treasurer and its only woman member in the 1960s.

No one accused the Exchange of an overly heavy regulatory touch. Missing a meeting would cost you $0.50. Late to a securities auction? Fork over $0.25. Indecorous conduct carried the biggest fine of all: $1.00.

In the early 1970s, one of the members announced that his firm wasn't going to continue to pay dues and support the exchange financially, so that was the end of the exchange. If he hadn't withdrawn support, I've been told, Richmond might have held on to claim one of the last of the nation's independent stock exchanges.

✌

One of the largest stockbrokers in the world traces its origins to Richmond. Said who? Someone who should know: Donald Regan, former chairman of Merrill Lynch and later Secretary of the Treasury and chief of staff to President Ronald Reagan.[4]

The lineage started with cotton trader Gwathmey & Co., which began in Richmond in 1820. In 1926, Gwathmey merged with E. A. Pierce, the nation's largest broker at the time, which a decade later merged with Merrill Lynch.

Merrill was proud enough of its Richmond genesis that for years the sign outside of its former building in Washington, D.C., proclaimed:

BUSINESS

ORIGINALLY ESTABLISHED

IN RICHMOND, VA

1820

The Gwathmey & Co. cotton trading operation may have vanished with time, and other cities may claim to be the birthplace of Merrill Lynch, but who's going to argue with the chairman of the board?

✌

As the 1960s came to a close, it was not imagined in Richmond that discount stockbrokers would someday upend the century-old way of trading stocks through family-run Main Street firms. Nor was it predicted that a partner of one of the family-run firms would be the one to start the city's first discount broker.

Patteson Branch, Sr., came home from World War II and helped form Branch & Company, a New York Stock Exchange member firm, based in the Branch Building on Main Street. By then, the Branch name had been prominent in Virginia's business circles for a century. Branch & Company was a successor to the family's investment business, which had separated from its banking operations during the Depression.

Patteson Branch's great-grandfather, Thomas Branch, ran several financial and commercial enterprises dating to the 1830s, and in 1870 in Richmond founded Merchants National Bank, a forerunner to First & Merchants Bank. (The vice president and second-largest shareholder of Merchants National was Frederic Scott, Thomas Branch's son-in-law, who would later found Scott & Stringfellow.)

Branch & Company disbanded in the 1970s, and Mr. Branch opened the doors to discount broker Exchange Services, Inc., in 1979. Far ahead of his time, he foresaw the unbundling of traditional brokerage services: portfolio analysis, safekeeping and transfer of securities, investment advice, and trading. Concentrating on the latter (charging just an eighth of a point a share), and employing effective advertising and sophisticated back-office software, Exchange Services was a familiar name to Richmond investors.

Exchange Services disappeared from the scene in 1992, when it was acquired by one of the largest national discount brokers, Quick & Reilly Group, Inc.[5]

In his foreword to David D. Ryan's captivating 1969 photographic essay of East Main Street, Fletcher Cox, Jr., wrote:

> There is a kind of excitement here [Ninth and Main Streets] that does not exist anywhere else in Richmond. It is the big time, the big city, tied by computers and wires to the stock exchanges, linked by importers and exporters to much of the world. There are deliveries and shipments, encounters and presentations on the sidewalks, cosmopolitan food and drinks in the Bull & Bear Club atop the Fidelity Building or the Downtown Club on the top floor of the Ross Building.[6]

By the 1980s and 1990s, Richmond's money business was wired to the rest of the world in a way unthinkable in 1969. The 2000s brought even faster computers and wires, more commerce, more restaurants, and bigger and more impressive buildings. True, Main Street today may not be "The Wall Street of the South" as described in days past, but even the original Wall Street isn't Wall Street anymore. A former colleague notes, with regret and just a bit of exaggeration, the once-dynamic floor of the New York Stock Exchange seems reduced to part TV studio, part venue for wine tastings.

Although Main Street did have one or two shady actors and a trace of indecorous conduct in the 1980s and 1990s, our storytellers describe their peers, overwhelmingly, as honorable and hard-working. Says Tom Gayner:

> *Business people around here tend to be more interested in doing than talking. Richmond oftentimes has quiet, understated people. They're not going to toot their own horn or call attention to themselves. That's admirable. It's a mark of humility and grace and someone who's concerned about other people. But the cost of that is sometimes stories get lost that are worth telling.*

What follows are stories worth hearing.

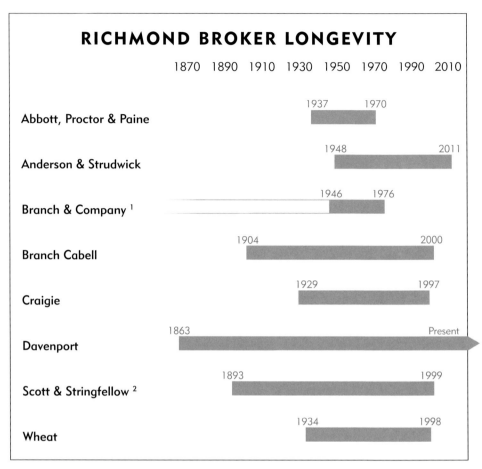

RICHMOND BROKER LONGEVITY

[1] Branch & Company, founded 1946, was successor to Thomas Branch and Brother, founded 1836.

[2] Acquired by BB&T in 1999; known as "BB&T Scott & Stringfellow" today.

Sources: *Richmond Times-Dispatch;*
Richmond News Leader; Virginia Historical
Society; Richmond Public Library;
company reports; www.bestbusinesspa.com

RICHMOND BANKS' EVOLUTION

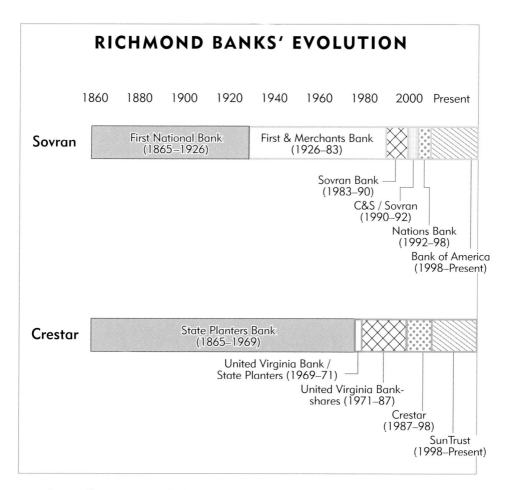

Sources: Company reports; *Wash-
ington Post*; Leigh Williams, *They
Faced the Future*; Library of Virginia
Dictionary of Virginia Biography

THE INTERVIEWS

I

THE CHAIRMAN

S. BUFORD SCOTT

Buford Scott, philanthropist and chairman of Scott & Stringfellow, Inc., has worked on Main Street for sixty-plus years. There's not enough space here to list his many volunteer and charitable endeavors, the boards and investment committees he has joined, and the awards he has received. When you talk to Buford, you can't help but be energized by his optimism, graciousness, and sense of humor. "I have too many blessings to ever be depressed."

My family has a tradition in the business, in that my grandfather started the firm in 1893 and my father became the senior partner when my grandfather died in 1939. When I was at the University of Virginia, I was a member of St. Paul's Episcopal Church in Richmond and interested in the Episcopal ministry. But of course I had a family heritage in the investment business, so my father arranged for me to work for two summers for St. Paul's. The director and the associate director were Bob Brown, later Bishop of Arkansas, and his right-hand man Holt Souder, who later became rector of St. Mary's Church in the west end of town.

I really appreciated the two summers I spent at St. Paul's Church, doing whatever jobs they had for me. Both Bob Brown and Holt Souder understood that in exchange for my working there, they were to give me some exposure to what life in the ministry was like. I remember working for a week at the MCV with the minister who was in charge of patients there. It gave me exposure to what being a minister to hospital patients was like.

One of the places I worked was St. Andrew's Church with a man named Harry Baldwin. He worked with people from a disadvantaged area of town, so that gave me additional exposure. Then I graduated from the University of Virginia in June 1955 and went to work for Scott & Stringfellow for seven months.

In those days, young men were required to be involved with the military. You could either be drafted, or you could volunteer for service. So I volunteered for service in early 1956. I went to basic training in Fort Jackson, South Carolina, for eight weeks, and apparently did very well on the rifle range and on some other tests they gave me.

Then one day the sergeant came up and asked if I would be interested in the Counter Intelligence Corps. I said yes and ended up at Fort Holabird just outside of Baltimore with a group of men. (We were all men at that time; there were no women.) We took another eight weeks of basic training to prepare us for the Counter Intelligence Corps.

The next question was, where would I be assigned? I was in the First Army area, which was headquartered at Fort George C. Meade, Maryland. I was told to show up at a certain time on a certain morning and be prepared to go wherever I was going to be assigned. I drove up from Richmond, and a very nice fellow—a sergeant—said they had two openings, one in Toledo and one in Richmond. He asked my preference, and I chose Richmond.

When I had left home that morning for Fort Meade in the 1955 Buick Special that my father gave me as a graduation present, I said to my father and mother that I didn't know when I'd see them again. When I drove back into the driveway that evening for dinner, I said, "Here I am. I'll be living at home and investigating my friends in Richmond for the rest of my time in the Army."

When my time in the Army was winding down, I went to Bob Brown, the man I'd worked for at St. Paul's, and told him that I had to make a decision as to whether to go into the ministry or whether to go into the investment business and would he help me.

He said, "Certainly. I think you would make a very good minister. And of course if you enter the ministry, you will have to give up your family's heritage in the investment business. If you become a stockbroker, remember that the church sometimes needs good laypeople as much, if not more, than good ordained people. And very often the ministry of a layperson can be as strong, if not stronger, than the ministry of an ordained person." I thought that was good advice, so I took a job at Scott & Stringfellow on the eighteenth of May 1958, having completed the two years of Army service and gaining at least some exposure to what the investment business was like.

My first job at Scott & Stringfellow was as a board boy. I don't know whether you remember the blackboard in our office at Ninth and Main.

The job of the board boys was to distribute the mail in the morning and then run off copies of something called the morning wire, which came from our New York correspondent Clark, Dodge & Co. We then distributed the morning wire around the office and to local banks and law firms so they would know what to expect in the market that day or what had happened the day before. Then when the market opened, the board boys were expected to be on duty and to indicate prices of stocks on the board so that our customers could come in and see what was going on in the market.

The real sport of each day was to see how many of the stocks we could open before noon. That was a lot of fun. We were quoting all New York Stock Exchange stocks on our board. We had another ticker that had American Stock Exchange stocks. There would be cheers when we opened all the stocks on our board. In those days the market opened at ten o'clock and closed at four o'clock. And we board boys kept the board up to date until the market closed. Then we went back to delivering mail and finishing up whatever had to be done in the mailroom. That was what life as a board boy was like.

After six months or so, they put me in the *cage.* I'm sure you don't remember the cage, because I think it was gone by your time. The cage was where we would receive securities that people had sold. We would give them a receipt and then send the securities off to wherever they had to go. It wasn't like transactions today. Back then, if you sold a hundred shares of General Motors, you had to receive the shares from the customer and send them off to whatever broker bought them.

One day my father, who was on the investment committee of the First & Merchants Bank, was coming out of a meeting with his friend Floyd Gottwald, who at that time ran a company called Albemarle Paper. Mr. Gottwald said to my father, "Is young Buford any good?" My father said, "I don't know. How do you tell?" Mr. Gottwald said, "Give him more responsibility than he can handle, and you'll be able to tell right quickly." So my father called me in the next morning and said, "We're going to make you a partner in the firm." They did, and apparently it worked out all right. That was 1960. Freddie Bocock later became a partner, and then others did, including Henry Spalding and Darrell Meade.

The biggest investment firm in Richmond was Abbott, Proctor & Paine. While they had an office in downtown Richmond, they also had probably five or six other offices around the state. A few years later, bad times came along in the business, and Abbott, Procter & Paine was purchased by Paine Webber.

Paine Webber did not want the smaller offices. This was 1970, as I well remember. We were offered the opportunity to buy a number of Abbott, Procter & Paine offices, taking over assets and employees. My father was not in favor of doing that, but by then we had brought in a number of other younger partners like Freddie Bocock and Henry Spalding. Joe Muldowney, an older man, was also one of our partners. Father appointed us to the executive committee. He said, "I want you younger men to take over the control of the firm, and I just want to be kept informed." We said that was fine with us. Everything went along smoothly until we decided to buy the three offices from Abbott, Proctor & Paine.

So I told my father, who was spending more and more time at his home on Cary Street Road, that we'd like to come talk to him about buying some offices. The executive committee wanted to do it, and we wanted to keep him informed.

We went to see him early one morning to inform him of the purchase of these offices from Abbott, Proctor & Paine. Father said he didn't approve of it. I said, "Father, you told us that you would go along with anything that we thought made sense. You only just wanted to be kept informed, and we are here to inform you that we're buying these offices." He said, "You can't do that." So I replied that I was resigning from the firm. Got up, walked out.

At that time, I was representing the firm in the Securities Industry Association, and Susie and I planned to take the train later that morning to an SIA meeting in Boca Raton. Susie was waiting in a taxi. I came out and told her that we weren't going to Florida, that I just resigned from the firm. We thought we might as well go somewhere, so we made a reservation at the Williamsburg Inn. We got in our car and drove to Williamsburg.

The word got out right quickly that Buford had resigned from the firm. Father's wonderful partner, Walter Robertson, and he were very close friends. They'd been partners together for many years. Mr. Robertson said to my father, "You're making a big mistake. Do whatever you can to get Buford back into the firm again." Mr. Robertson and I had a talk. He said my father wanted me back, to go by his house, and he'd talk to me on Monday morning. So I did that. My father said, "I made a mistake. I should not have gone against my agreement to let you all run the firm, and I'd like you to come back again." I said I would. That's the worst experience I've ever had in the business. I went back to work the next morning, and most people never even knew it happened.

The purchase of those three offices from Abbott, Proctor & Paine was the beginning of the expansion of the firm. Little by little, we were able to acquire other offices. The biggest acquisition was Investment Corporation of Virginia, located in Norfolk, with a lot of talented people. My guess is they had twenty to twenty-five people working for them.

That was the biggest jump we made. We acquired a firm in North Carolina, which gave us a presence down there. Then, from time to time, we would acquire other firms. It got to the point where I, who at that time was chairman and CEO of the firm, realized that the firm needed full-time management, because I was also handling accounts. So we decided to hire a full-time executive, Frank Pineno. Frank became our chief executive officer and helped us expand the firm. I think Frank was the one responsible for our acquiring the office in Norfolk. Frank was a great success. Why did he leave? I think he wanted to focus more on research than running a brokerage firm. And a couple of people who were in our research department left with him to form their own firm.

Our initial public offering in 1987 came about because we were keeping in touch with what other companies were doing, and our partners had almost all of their assets invested in the firm. We noticed a number of other investment firms of our size were going public. We looked into it and decided that it made sense for our owners and our clients for us to have stock in the hands of the public.

It worked out fine. My father and I had gotten to know a number of people in the business across the country. One was Jim Kellogg, who was one of the most influential men on Wall Street and sat on the board of governors of the New York Stock Exchange. He was a good friend of my father's. When my father became quite ill, Mr. Kellogg, God bless him, flew down to Richmond and brought this medallion[7] to my father.

There was a close relationship between the Scott and the Kellogg families, and before long we realized that Spear, Leeds & Kellogg (Mr. Kellogg's firm) was acquiring our stock. They became the largest shareholder outside of the management of the firm. I got to know young Peter Kellogg, Jim Kellogg's son, and we remain friends to this day. Peter Kellogg realized that the investment business was changing, and that the smaller firms had a lot of potential. So he bought stock in a lot of the regional firms, including ours. I think he made a lot of money as the regional firms then were absorbed by major Wall Street firms.

Everything was going fine in the late 90s. We were making money and paying dividends. Our stock price was appreciating. Banks started approaching us to see if we were interested in selling the firm. For over a year, the board determined independence was our best strategy.

Time went by, and ultimately, we had discussions with BB&T leading to a merger in 1999. We sold for over three times book value, and as far as we know, it was the best price any small firm received.

John Allison, chairman and chief executive officer of BB&T, told us we knew how to run a brokerage firm, and they knew how to run a bank. We would keep running our brokerage firm, and they would keep running their bank, and we'll see how we can do business together. It hasn't worked out exactly that way all the time, but pretty close, because they are honorable people. I think it has been the most successful combination of a bank and a brokerage firm in the country. And, of course, we were happy with the wealth we created for our shareholders.

I recall merger discussions with Davenport years before the BB&T deal . . .

Yes, the proposed merger with Davenport was before we entered into any relationship with BB&T. We knew the leaders of Davenport, and they knew us, and we both had respect for each other. We had a series of meetings and finally decided that we would combine the two firms. Our board got together and voted to approve the merger. I was going to New Jersey, where I was the advisor to a company up there, and Davenport's board was going to meet that afternoon or evening and hopefully approve the merger too. The next morning, I got a call from Henry Valentine, who said he was horribly embarrassed to make the call, but his board did not approve the merger. That really surprised me. It had been entirely unexpected. I said, "Okay, Henry. We'll still find ways to work together and be friends." I then informed our board that the merger had not been approved. Davenport went their own way, and we went our own way.

Before I leave, Mr. Scott recounts a wonderful poem he wrote in 1996, "Whiskey Sour":

If you wish to wile away an hour
Do it with a whiskey sour.
If you wish to entertain a friend
Lemon and whiskey is the blend.
If you wish to entertain a crowd
Whiskey sours will make you proud.
Whiskey sours are very good
To liven up the neighborhood.
If you want to make the party bigger—
Put more whiskey in the jigger.
The truth is sours are the best
After two or three you need a nest!
So here's a toast we hope you think
To whiskey sours our favorite drink!

The recipe: one can frozen lemonade, one can water, and sour mash bourbon (two cans for a gathering of mostly ladies, three cans for a mixed crowd, or four cans if mostly men).

II

THE MONEY MANAGERS

WILLIAM J. LONGAN

Bill is a Senior Investment Advisor with SunTrust Bank. He completed the Certified Investment Management Analyst program at the Wharton School and is a director with SunTrust's Foundations and Endowments Specialty Practice. He has served on the Boards of Riverside School, Robert E. Lee Council of the Boy Scouts of America, and the Historic Richmond Foundation, along with a leadership position in The Society of the Cincinnati (Virginia). An avid reader, historian, student of the financial markets, outdoorsman, and Nascar fan, a discourse by Bill on any subject is literate, original, and usually very humorous.

I graduated from Carolina in '76 and after a while went to work for Anderson & Strudwick in the brokerage business. I worked for Charlie Mills, who was an interesting guy with a remarkable work ethic. From the beginning, I saw some important things in the financial services industry that I consider mileposts.

One was deregulation and elimination of fixed commissions. I got into the brokerage business two or three years after the New York Stock Exchange was no longer allowed to set commission rates. Prior to that, the New York Stock Exchange set commissions. There was no negotiation. Deregulation created the first discount brokerage firms, a major change in the brokerage business.

Previously, if you bought a hundred shares of VEPCO at Davenport or Anderson & Strudwick or Scott & Stringfellow or Merrill Lynch, the New York Stock Exchange set commission rates, which, based on today's standards, were astronomically higher than they are now. So that certainly changed the landscape of the brokerage business.

A second milepost was the repeal of the Glass-Steagall Act in 1999. Prior to its repeal, there was a stone wall between commercial banking and investment banking. Commercial banks could not participate in certain types of underwriting activities.

Glass-Steagall's origins date to the 1920s and 1930s. A lot of people don't realize that banks used to go out of business. And when banks went out of business prior to the 1920s and 1930s, depositors lost their money. That's inconceivable today. But a hundred years ago, you wanted to bank with a strong bank because that meant the integrity of your deposit was strong.

One of the reasons that we regulated banks even before the Great Depression was that a lot of lending was tied to a much bigger agricultural economy, and the agricultural economy rose and fell, failed and prospered, based upon crop cycles. If you had a bad crop or a drought, all of a sudden a lot of local banks would go out of business, because a lot of their lending was levered back to the agricultural economy.

When I got into the business, because of Glass-Steagall, banks could underwrite municipal finance, but not corporate deals. There was a lot they couldn't do. They certainly could not own seats in the New York Stock Exchange. And they couldn't be market makers or run specialist firms.

When Glass-Steagall was repealed, the financial services industry was fundamentally changed in a way that I have come, after 2008, to feel was really damaging. The repeal goes back to Sandy Weill, the CEO of Citibank, badgering Congress, saying he wanted a chance to be as profitable as Intel and Microsoft. If they would let him get into the investment banking business, he could be as profitable as those companies. If he could be that profitable, then look how much better he could serve the credit needs of every single community he was working with.

Well as it turns out, it was an absolute train wreck. All we have to look at is what happened in 2008. I believe Weill says today that the repeal was a mistake, and that Glass-Steagall should be reinstituted.

A third big change was interstate banking. I look out my window today and I see two big national banks. When I looked out this window twenty years ago, I would've seen maybe four banks or more. But today there's only the one that I'm sitting in, and the two that I can see. So what was that all about?

United Virginia Bank, a predecessor of the bank that I work for, was one of the pioneers in branch banking. We don't see branch banking as a big deal today. We don't give it a second thought. But the patriarch of United Virginia Bank was one of the people who played a very big leadership role in Virginia adopting branch banking, which the General Assembly was extremely tentative about and hesitant to consider.

Why the resistance to branch banking? Well, who was going to serve the credit needs of Crewe, Virginia? Who's going to serve the credit needs of Pound, Virginia? Who's going to serve the credit needs of Galax? Other than the Bank of Crewe or the Bank of Pound or the Bank of Galax. And if the credit needs for Galax, Virginia, are being decided in the metropolis of Roanoke, then you're harming the commerce in Galax. We need to have the credit decisions made locally, the argument went.

So Mr. Wilkinson[8] was one of the ones who said this is antiquated and out of date; it does not imperil commerce in the Commonwealth. Branch banking started to get under way in the late sixties and early seventies, but it was very timid and very slow because opponents thought it jeopardized business and commerce and credit availability in rural areas.

North Carolina had been light years ahead in adopting branch banking, so the large North Carolina banks learned how to do mergers and acquisitions. That's why today, when I look out my window, I see two banks with headquarters in Charlotte. That profoundly changed the look of financial services in Virginia.

Those milestone events must have changed the character of Main Street.

With the advent of discount brokerage firms, a lot of profitability disappeared. When I got into the business, we would have a verbal understanding with a customer that they got 20 percent off or 30 percent off or X number of cents per share. Ten years earlier, I would not have seen that because there was no negotiating of commissions. If you bought one hundred shares of IBM, you paid the same commission rate regardless of where you bought it. So a big part of the profitability picture started to change.

When I think back to Anderson & Strudwick where I worked, this little four-block zone on Main Street was called the Wall Street of the South. That sounds kind of corny and parochial, but in many ways it was a little microcosm of Wall Street, in a provincial way.

You had big, prominent, highly regarded trust departments, most of which were affiliated with big commercial banks, where the wealthy and well-heeled had their assets managed. You had the trust department at United Virginia Bank, which was called the J. P. Morgan of the South. You had a big, prominent trust department at F&M, which became Bank of America. You had a big trust department at what became Central Fidelity, which started out as Central National before it merged with a bank in Lynchburg.

So you had these three big trust departments, and they played important and powerful roles. Then you had brokerage firms that were in a very different business, a transactional business. They were investment bankers on two levels. One was through corporate finance, meaning raising capital for for-profit organizations. They also played a big role in municipal finance.

You had Wheat with a large municipal finance operation, as did Scott & Stringfellow and Davenport. Those were the big three. And Anderson & Strudwick to a much smaller degree. Then there were the wire houses—Dean Witter Reynolds, Paine Webber, Merrill Lynch.

You had Craigie, which was known as a municipal finance shop. That's who they were and what they did. They did municipal finance. Later, you could buy a stock as well as a bond there.

Banks and the brokerage firms were able to compete for municipal finance business, but not for private company finance. Commercial business was part of the brokers' franchise before the repeal of Glass-Steagall. Big trust departments and brokerage firms had separate identities. With the repeal of Glass-Steagall, those identities were lost.

What are your recollections of the Crash of '87?

I remember the day very well. The preceding week had been rough. That Friday had been a bad day. Several things were going on. One was the advent of a lot of derivatives that were still very new, where people didn't understand the consequences.

This gets back to the elimination of fixed commission rates, which caused brokerage firms to have to come up with more and more gizmos to make up for lost revenue. The Chicago Board Options Exchange traded options on individual stocks, and later options on indexes; the Chicago Mercantile Exchange started trading futures contracts on the S&P 500. And it doesn't take Wall Street very long to figure out that there are arbitrage opportunities between the futures contract and the underlying security.

All of this kind of came together Monday morning in the perfect storm. I was running a derivatives-intensive program that did not envision an environment like the one we walked into, where the stock market opened down two hundred points. It was a discontinuous market. People think when IBM closes at 150, it opens up the next day at 150. Well, Friday IBM closed at 150 and opened up on Monday at 139. And it wasn't just one stock doing that; it was the entire market.

So you had the role of derivatives, and also a dynamic hedging strategy called portfolio insurance, which was vended by consulting firms to large pension plans, large state retirement plans, and large college and university endowment funds.

I had no idea if I had a job the next day. I couldn't put one foot in front of the other. The nature of the investments I was responsible for were not designed in a way that in any fashion envisioned an event like that. It was a bad day investment-wise for me.

As it turns out, I had done a little business with a broker at a big New York firm who absolutely saw it coming. He was an exceptionally smart guy. He was very opinionated. "This isn't real. This isn't going to last. This is a bunch of baloney and it's all going to fall apart, and I have a pretty good idea of how that's going to happen." Legend has it he bought hundreds of S&P puts at a sixteenth, at a thirty-second, and on that one day became an enormously wealthy man. Immediately quit, bought a great big Suburban, and moved his family to Wyoming. That's the legend. That's the wives' tale. What happened, I don't know. But Barton Biggs wrote a fun article about him and what happened that day.

I've seen some real characters when I was in the brokerage business. I remember one guy—I don't know if he's still around—who would take wild option positions on Friday afternoons and bail out of them on Mondays. And the branch manager would just hold his breath all weekend, hoping he could pay for them.

I was very new in the business, and I remember how once a month the branch manager would have these panic attacks about whether or not this guy would pay for these extremely high-risk options transactions. Then one weekend, the branch manager just had it, and he took the customer out of the trades at some big loss because he was scared he wasn't going to pay for them.

What's your outlook for the financial services industry now?

I think we're having our Amazon moment.

What is an Amazon moment?

It's a competitive threat that nobody sees coming. It's a bit of a black swan. If you ask the average American retailer today, "Tell me about Amazon," their feeling about the business that they're in is very different today than it was five years ago. And I think financial services is having its Amazon moment.

I think we're starting to see it with competitive threats from Vanguard, for instance. People don't want to pay for bells and whistles if they don't feel like they need bells and whistles. And Vanguard has become quite skilled in persuading people you don't need a lot of superfluous trimmings that you're paying a lot of money for.

So I think the competitive landscape continues to change and continues to evolve. I doubt if my son or daughter will ever go into a bank branch. And if they do, it would be once every five years. Look at the capital overhead that banks have for branches. How people access the financial markets is very different today. It's done online. Perhaps it's done through an 800 number.

The models that I knew when I came into the business are long gone. They don't exist anymore. And I think that's going to continue to change, and change a lot.

MICHAEL M. VIA

Mike manages the Baymount (SMA) Portfolios with Capital Securities Manage-ment, Inc. His office now is in Tampa, Florida. When Mike became director of research at Anderson & Strudwick, Richmond's stock analysts focused on local companies almost exclusively, leaving national research to their New York cor-respondents. Mike emphasized superior stock selection, regardless of geography, period. I recall an institutional investor asking him how, without underwriting a lot of IPOs, a small firm like Anderson & Strudwick could make money. His reply: "We buy stocks that go up."

I had graduated from the University of Virginia and was working in an accounting capacity at the university's hospital in Charlottesville in 1980. I had a lot of friends who were working in Richmond, so that gave me a way to share an apartment and try the financial business in Rich-mond without making a major financial commitment.

Richmond had several local firms that were members of the New York Stock Exchange, the most in any city in the country outside of New York, I believe. It was an old-school, old-time financial center.

Not being from Richmond, I found it was rather tough to get a job in the financial area. The one thing that got me through the door at Branch, Cabell was the fact that I'd graduated from—as we called it— "The University." The partner at the time who was in charge of hiring trainees attended the University of Virginia. So I started there as a trainee.

Branch, Cabell was a full-service firm that also specialized in small-cap and micro-cap over-the-counter stocks. It was a proprietary research effort, headed by some really talented people—maybe a little bit more outside the box than a lot of people might have been used to. The strategy attracted a strong client base and business was good.

I always wanted to work in a structure like Branch, Cabell's, which I felt had more of an entrepreneurial spirit than some of the other firms. As such, I got an opportunity to do some research and get my feet wet. But I didn't know where that was going to go . . . sales were not my favor-ite thing, and they still really wanted me to open accounts and do retail business.

I knew some guys who went to Anderson & Strudwick for various reasons, and they offered me an opportunity to do research on a more fo-cused basis. As with a lot of firms, the job would still involve some sales, obviously. When I got there, A&S had a fairly modest but more conventional research effort. They were using material they received from their New York correspondents, supplemented by original material from their own staff.

A lot of firms would publish research reports on local, Virginia companies. Davenport had a niche in that, as did Scott & Stringfellow—everybody in Richmond was doing it to some degree. I was just interested in finding stocks that went up. If it was a small company based in California, so be it. So we went with that philosophy and got some genuine interest among the brokers in the firm.

The sales manager made the suggestion that I show my research to institutions, which I did. I remember vividly my first appointment with the special situations portfolio manager at the Bank of New York. I thought that was a good start, and it was, for a twenty-something-year-old kid.

Over the next several years, from the ground up, we started an institutional research and sales effort. We developed a network of buy-side funds and money managers around the country in the small cap value area, which was a pretty well-defined investment community in the mid to late '80s and into the '90s. That was our niche. We received a lot of financial press exposure and did very well with the strategy. I ended up spending twenty years at Anderson & Strudwick.

It's interesting how the regulatory climate changed from the 1980s to the 2000s, after a number of high-profile stock collapses (such as Enron) and various changes in Washington. For instance, back then it was commonplace for analysts to have private one-on-one contacts with companies that would not be permitted today.

Today, just about all companies conduct conference calls when they announce earnings. But even large companies didn't do it as a matter of policy until the 2000s. We arranged for some of our smaller companies to hold conference calls, and we would hook up eight or ten institutional accounts on the phone that we were either working with or trying to work with. We would conduct our own conference calls with management after earnings announcements. It was just the companies, the institutional investors that we invited, and us. It wasn't a publicly available call. That really wasn't done when we started, so I think we kind of pioneered it.

On the institutional side, we would go to New York or wherever, and we would take management teams around to various buy-side managers. You really get to know people pretty well when you're spending downtime with them on multi-day road trips. I remember once we were taking around the CEO of a manufactured housing company. He was kind of a good old boy from North Texas. We were walking across the street in New York, where, as you know, you don't lollygag. But he saw a dime on the ground and stopped to pick it up and put it in his pocket. It struck me as very interesting and amusing. This guy was that frugal. He was wealthy, but he's stopping in the middle of traffic in New York to pick up a dime out of the street. You learn things about people's character and that can come in handy sometimes in sales pitches.

What about activities outside of the office in Richmond?

The brokerage firms in Richmond in the 1980s and 1990s competed with each other for customers. And they would compete for brokers too, of course. They'd also compete in sports. There was a highly popular coed brokerage softball league. For a number of years, we also had a volleyball league through the YMCA, where even the Federal Reserve Bank fielded a team. So there was a lot of healthy play time among the financial people.

Just like New York and everywhere else I suppose, there was also happy hour after work. There were a number of popular spots that people frequented. Some of the firms would congregate in different places and sometimes intermingle. A few of the location names that stick out would be Matt's British Pub, The Tobacco Company, Sam Miller's Exchange Café, and W. T. O'Malley's. Those were the big ones. I remember we went to the Shockoe Slip Café after work on Black Monday in 1987 to drown in our sorrows.

How was work that day?

Well, I was at my desk, and I remember I called my mom. I would never call my mom from my desk at work, but that day you kind of needed your blanket and your mommy. Everybody was just kind of sitting there. The next day *Investor's Business Daily* quoted a market technician who said, "A seismologist is least busy during an earthquake." That's pretty much where we were.

After work we went to the bar. It was a pretty big contingent of Anderson & Strudwick people. After a while a senior officer came strolling in. He had come to Anderson & Strudwick from Scott & Stringfellow a year or so before. He was a big producer, a big research guy, and he was always generous. He just plopped down at the table, laughed and said, "Sorry guys, I'm not buying today!"

What were some notable market-moving events that you recall?

Shortly after I was out of training and registered in 1981, President Reagan was shot and seriously wounded. While this was a shocking event for everyone, it was particularly hard for the investment community. Reagan had run on a very pro-business, low-tax platform and that registered well with Wall Street and Main Street. In 1981, we didn't have a single TV in the Branch, Cabell office. The shooting occurred in the early afternoon and the stock market immediately headed lower and closed early. With only the Dow Jones news wire at the office, a group of us walked down to the Bull & Bear Club, then located at the Fidelity Building at Ninth and Main, to watch the live TV coverage.

The first Gulf War also stands out in my mind for a number of reasons. After Iraq invaded Kuwait in August 1990, world equity markets reflected the danger and uncertainty surrounding the potential for war, a prolonged oil crisis, and an inevitable economic downturn. The S&P 500 dropped around 15% from July to October 1990. The resulting slump in our business made for precarious times for many firms. I recall a day when Secretary of State James Baker met with Iraqi Foreign Minister Tariq Aziz for a last ditch effort to avert war. The meeting yielded nothing, and the market plunged. As I looked out of the window from the Anderson & Strudwick office in the old Plantation House building, I could see a fast moving CSX train hauling an endless stream of army tanks and heavy equipment. It was a bleak day indeed.

How has the business changed?

Obviously, it's changed from 1980 through today in a number of ways. But I think if you look at the year 1980, if you walked into Branch, Cabell, as I did, or Scott & Stringfellow, you walked into buildings that had been brokerage firm offices going back to the early 1900s, or before.

You would walk in from the street into what was called the board room. In this case, the board room was not for the board of directors or for board meetings. It was a common area with the receptionist near the front door, a room where you had the ticker tape.

At Branch, Cabell, they still had the blackboards on the wall that were used for stock and bond quotes. In the old days they would have *board boys* who would write the prices with chalk. There were about a dozen wooden chairs scattered around the room filled with old retired men in suits, maybe smoking a cigar, maybe asleep or whatever, watching the tape. Back then we did have the Bunker Ramo quote machines with a screen that was about four inches wide over in the corner, but the old men didn't use that. They would just sit and watch the tape.

An older gentleman, a senior partner, was the only broker who had a desk in the board room. Everybody else had their desks in various different places—the bullpen or a private office. But he sat in the board room where the tape was. He had a Bunker Ramo quote machine on his desk, but it was always turned off. He had no use for it. He said that he could tell exactly what the Dow was doing just by watching the tape. And pretty much that's what all those guys did. I'm sure at Scott & Stringfellow it was the same thing.

When you walked in there, you saw all of that. When you think about it, all of the guys in suits, the ticker tape, all of this stuff, would have looked exactly the same in 1915. All of that technology, all of what those people were doing, was pretty much unchanged. Nothing had changed from 1915 until 1980. Not one thing.

Now, talking about the 1980s and 1990s, that's when you started to see radical change, which was initially wrought by technology. In 1980 you had the Bunker Ramo and hand-written order tickets. Not long after that you had sophisticated quote systems and electronic trading platforms. Shortly after 1980, you could readily obtain reams of information through such avenues as the Financial News Network, which was later bought by CNBC. All of a sudden, board rooms became obsolete. They kicked the old guys out. They divided the board room into cubicles. Nothing had changed in sixty years. Then, in just ten short years, things changed dramatically. Those changes were logistical, technological, and psychological. I believe that period was a bridge between the old school and the modern era.

While there has obviously been a lot of change since the 1990s, a lot of it could just be considered refinements. There's algorithmic trading, ETFs, and hedge funds that trade hedge funds. The board rooms are gone, family firms are gone, and brokers now work for what used to be called a wire house. Now I guess you'd just call them banks.

What's an interesting memory from your start at Branch, Cabell?

In the early 1980s we were at the Christmas party at a partner's home in the West End of Richmond. I was chatting with the senior partner who had his desk in the board room. He began as a clerk in the late '20s. He had pedaled his bicycle around Richmond to collect margin calls in 1929.

There's a buffet table with a huge tray of ham and shrimp. He's standing there, and all of a sudden he reaches over and grabs a handful of ham, stuffs it into his mouth, and looks at me and says, "Son, this is how we eat ham in Virginia." There's nothing I could do except grab a handful myself and join him. I'm not quite sure what the other guests thought of our behavior. ◼

ERWIN H. WILL, JR.

Erwin was chief investment officer of the Virginia Retirement System and founder of Capitoline Investment Management, among his other senior executive positions. He was a director of The Community Foundation Serving Richmond and Central Virginia. Erwin also served as chief investment officer of the West Virginia University Foundation, Inc. Our conversation took place in a sunny meeting room in Erwin's Westminster Canterbury residence. Considering his long and successful career on Main Street, it's no surprise that several other people interviewed for this book worked for him at one point or another. They all had fond and positive recollections of him.

I started with Provident Mutual Life Insurance Company in Philadelphia in 1956, after graduating from the University of Virginia. I stayed there two years. Harvie Wilkinson of State Planters Bank hired me in the investment department in Richmond. My future boss, with whom I worked for ten years, was Jack Jennings, who later became head of the banking system which evolved from State Planters to United Virginia Bank to Crestar, and eventually to SunTrust.

One of my assignments when I came on board in 1958 was the life and casualty insurance industry. I came across a company called General Reinsurance, and I couldn't believe how profitable it was and how few employees it had. So I went to the headquarters in New York City to talk to management. First of all, they didn't pay any dividend. They had good earnings, but didn't pay any dividend. They were such a small company in terms of personnel, but so big in reinsurance and profitability. How did they do it? The person I met with said they weren't going to pay any dividends, so don't buy the stock for a dividend. And the majority of stock was owned by Paul Mellon, who didn't need the income. I was very interested in the stock, so I presented it to our investment committee at the weekly meeting. The bank board made up most of the investment committee, which was a great advantage to me, because I got to know all the key board members personally.

The committee liked the idea, and we put it on our list of stocks to buy. Randy Cardozo, a portfolio manager, was managing part of the UVA endowment fund. He bought ten thousand shares. I thought, what have I done? Well, of course the stock did nothing but go up until Warren Buffett took it over.

Harvie Wilkinson always thought that the investment operation should be separate and independent from the trust operation, because he thought the managers would be more aggressive. I think he was right. So we had a separate investment operation at the bank. We not only provided investment services to the trust department, but also ran the bank's portfolio, and subsequently the municipal bond department, which started when Jack Howe and Mark Smith came over from Wheat in the early '60s.

I hired Doug Ludeman to head up the bank's bond portfolio and the municipal department. He subsequently became head of United Virginia Bank.

Capitoline was formed in the early '70s, to be distinct from the bank. Capitoline was a wholly owned subsidiary, with the thought that we could solicit business other than trust business, such as pension business and other types of endowment funds. That worked pretty well. C&S[9] in Atlanta was the only other bank that I knew of that had a subsidiary like ours.

We were fairly autonomous and well organized. We had four investment analysts and a manager, and a research head. Our research was a significant advantage. I think that helped us to do a better job for our customers. We had some very good people, like Charles Grant, who later worked at the Virginia Retirement System. Bates Chappell, who runs Kanawha Capital, was also at Capitoline, as was John Flippin from Lynchburg, who died a few years ago. We had our own marketing operations, with Greg Porter as head of marketing.

They became the Flippin, Bruce & Porter investment firm in Lynchburg?

Right. All three[10] worked for me. I tried to get Capitoline to become completely independent of the bank. In other words, we'd buy ourselves out. When that proposal was turned down by the bank, the three of them decided they'd go to Lynchburg and start their own business. They came to see me and discussed the whole thing. I understood why and what they were doing. I was not happy about it, but I understood.

How did you came up with the name Capitoline? Is it named after the hill in Rome?

Yes. We were trying to come up with a name, so we had people submit names. We narrowed them down to three, Capitoline being one,

and I don't remember the other two. Walt Turnbull, who was head of the
trust and investment area at that time and was going to be the chairman
of Capitoline, said put the three names in a hat, and the one picked out
would be the winner.

The next day he came in with a hat with three names in it. I picked
one out: Capitoline. Well, it turned out all three names in there were Capitoline, because that's the one he liked.

I left Capitoline at the end of '91. My wife, Mary, became terminally
ill in '90, so I took early retirement to take care of her. I'd been there thir-
ty-three years by then. But she only lived seventy-two days after being di-
agnosed. I was happy in retirement and wasn't anxious to go back to work.

I had been chairman of the board of the Virginia Retirement System
in the '70s, an interesting experience. Walter Craigie was Virginia state
treasurer, and he was the one who had me appointed chairman. The position had an eight-year term.

We made some significant and fruitful changes to the system, which
paid off. But then the retirement system experienced big turmoil in the
early '90s, when it looked like some people were going to be indicted.
The General Assembly terminated all board members and appointed new
ones.

Jimmy Wheat of Wheat, First Securities was chairman of the board
of the Virginia Retirement System at the time. He called me in March
1992 and said that nobody on the board knew anything about the retirement system; they were all new with no prior experience, so would I be a
consultant to them? I agreed, and he asked me to come down and work
out a contract with him.

The night before I was to go down to meet him for the contract, he
called and told me the board met that day and terminated the director. As
of the next day, I would be the new acting director.

I wasn't anxious to go to the retirement system because I knew they
had a lot of problems, and I knew things were not going well. I thought,
did I really want to jump into that morass? They talked me into it. I said
that I would do it for a short period until they hired someone new.

In May, when I'd been there about five weeks, Jeff Schapiro, who
had been tearing us apart in the newspaper, called me right after I became
acting director. One of the questions he asked me was how much were
they paying me. I asked him if I had to answer that question.

He replied that I didn't have to tell him, but personnel would tell him if I didn't. So I told him I was getting fifteen thousand dollars a month. But I was a contract employee, not an employee of the state. I had all the retirement benefits from the bank, and I didn't need those benefits.

Once I got there and saw the mess, it was pretty easy to see how it could be straightened out. It wasn't brain surgery; it was pretty straightforward. Just stop doing a lot of dumb things and use common sense. It didn't take long to turn it around and get it going in the right direction

Anyway, we had about three hundred employees in the administrative process who handled the pensions and benefits. I found that it was all administrative work, which I'm not very fond of. There were all kinds of personnel problems. I thought it was a nightmare.

So I had Glen Pond hired as the director, and he came in and straightened it all out. I told Jimmy Wheat now that we'd hired a director, he had to hire a chief investment officer.

But Jimmy said they weren't going to go through the hiring process again: "That was a nightmare. You're going to be the chief investment officer." I didn't know whether I wanted to do that or not.

Nancy Everett (who later went to General Motors) was there, and she was quite capable. She indicated that she would love to be the chief investment officer one day. But if they hired somebody else from outside to come in and do it, she'd never get a chance. If I stayed, she'd do the investment work and we'd work it out. I'd handle the board, and that type of thing.

I thought that was fine, and that it would work.

It did work out. They had been doing a lot of things that were dumb, and they were naive about a lot of things. We got it worked out. I was chief investment officer from 1994 to 2001. After I stepped down in 2001, I stayed on the investment committee for a period of three years.

What sort of changes did you make? What were they doing that you didn't like?

We were paying too much in fees. I'm cheap. I'm a great one on cost cutting. We got rid of a lot of excess managers and forced some fee reductions through other managers.

We had a private equity consultant that we were paying six to eight hundred thousand dollars a year, which I thought was ridiculous. The consultant called me from New York and said they'd like to come down and meet me, since I was the new head. Three of them came down, and we went to dinner and talked. They were knowledgeable people, but again, I didn't think we needed them.

About two weeks later, we got a bill from them for their travel expenses, their airplane tickets, the hotel rooms, and the dinner. You pay somebody six to eight hundred thousand dollars a year, and they send you a bill for their dinner? I thought that was the most ridiculous thing I had ever heard of.

I told the manager of our private equity area to terminate them. So at the end of their contract, we terminated them.

Did the retirement system manage any money in-house at that time?

Yes. We managed a little bit. But I was in favor of us managing more. So we built a staff to do that. I think it's been very fruitful. They've done a good job and saved an enormous amount in fees. I think it's good to have both in-house managers and some on the outside. It's worked well for the system.

When I went there in the early '90s, the trustees had an executive committee that I worked with. I got them to agree to let me work with three people rather than all the trustees so we could make decisions as we went along and not have to wait for a board meeting. The three were Jimmy Wheat, Charlie Walker, and Ed Burton from UVA. Ed Burton is a very knowledgeable, very outspoken person. I got along well with everybody, except on a couple of occasions.

We were all sitting there, the three of them and myself, and I told them that if I meet with you individually, what I tell you is what I'm going to tell him and tell him. It won't be two different stories. It's always going to be the same story. And it worked out well. The four of us did not see eye to eye on a lot of things, and I didn't want to get in the middle of a squabble.

One of the first things I looked at was the payroll. The investment people were getting state salaries, and raises of 2 percent or whatever it was. You can't hire qualified investment people on those salaries. It's not going to work. So we agreed to set up a separate salary scale for the investment people, which I think has been one of the keys to success.

And of course you've seen the salaries in the newspaper that some of those people are making. I didn't make anything like that when I was there. But it's deserved because we have some quality and knowledgeable investment people there. We had to compete with Wall Street for talent.

What kind of interaction did the Virginia Retirement System have with Richmond-based brokers?

We had some relationships. But it's difficult to have significant relationships because when we were buying or selling, we might invest five hundred million dollars in one day in a group of stocks. When you go to Branch, Cabell or any small firm and try to get them to compete based on commission and execution, it was very, very difficult. They couldn't compete in that volume. It's not like you're buying one hundred thousand shares of IBM. It's more like you're going to buy one hundred thousand shares of five hundred stocks. There were several New York firms that competed very vigorously for that business, so it was hard to do it locally.

Tell me some of your impressions of difficult markets.

The 1987 Crash started on Friday. Friday's market was lousy. It wasn't a disaster, but it was lousy. So I called a meeting for first thing Monday morning for all the investment people. We discussed how we would handle it with customers. Well, I didn't realize that Monday and Tuesday and Wednesday were also going to be awful. What we decided to do was have every portfolio manager call all their accounts and discuss it with them, which I think was the right thing to do. We didn't sell into the market. We didn't buy, initially, when the market was sliding. We did subsequent to that, but the market had hit the bottom and was turning when we started buying into it. It was an awful experience.

There was a bad market in 1971. In those days, you had the tickertape, which is the way you found out what was going on. When the market went down and volume went up, the tickertape couldn't keep up. So when the market closed at four o'clock, the tickertape kept running and running for several hours afterwards. You didn't know what final closing prices were. Most of the firms—certainly those in Richmond—had major administrative problems in processing trades. Some of the people stayed well past midnight trying to get it done. But it wasn't that bad in 1987. It could've been, but it wasn't. It's good they didn't have the tickertape then or we would still be sitting there.

I believe you were one of the early Chartered Financial Analysts®.

I was involved in the Financial Analyst Federation and was chairman of the national organization in 1981. We started the CFA program back in the '60s. I was in the first group that took all three exams. My CFA number is 880, and there are well over a couple hundred thousand now.

To get the program started, they initially grandfathered in a lot of people over a certain age. Then they said you had to take the Level I exam to become a CFA if you were a certain age and then the Level II exam if you were a younger age. And then if you were the youngest age, you had to take all three. Well, I was in the group that had to take all three.

The thing that interests me now is that if you looked at that first exam you'd say it wasn't tough. But what you're missing is there were no investment books available except Graham and Dodd. There wasn't the academic research that you have today. You were on your own, so to speak. I thought it was a great test in that the material was self-taught. Today you can read a book that teaches you. I think that was a big difference.

I used to grade those exams (they wanted investment people to grade the exams). It was two weeks every summer in Charlottesville. It wasn't easy, but it was enjoyable in that you got to meet a lot of people and make friends with people from all over the country.

What is your view on the trend today toward indexing versus active management?

I generally agree with that trend. I agree in indexing a significant portion of your portfolio and managing a separate portion in an active manner that you think may be more productive. I do think it's very difficult to beat the index year in and year out. I think for individuals, as they get older, indexing is more critical.

And for the big retirement systems, fees are very expensive. People can point to private equity and how successful they've been or how much money people have made in private equity, which is true. But what they don't tell you is if you're not in the top 10 or 20 percent of the best firms, you're not going to do well at all. The bottom 70 or 80 percent will underperform.

Any final thoughts on the business, looking back or looking forward?

As to where we're going, I don't know. I worry about the economics of Social Security and Medicare. To me, they're unsustainable economically, and it's just a matter of time before the guillotine falls. The population numbers are particularly disturbing in that many of the developed countries are no longer growing. Population growth, if there's any at all, is through immigration. Once you have a stagnant workforce, there's very little you can do to grow GDP. I think people are overlooking some very difficult issues. So I worry about the future for my children and grandchildren.

Looking back? I think my career was during a golden time in the investment community. I was very lucky, very fortunate. ◼

Austin is co-founder of Lowe, Brockenbrough & Company. He's been an active volunteer and philanthropist for years in many organizations, including the Boys and Girls Clubs of Metro Richmond, the Medical College of Virginia Foundation, the Christian Children's Fund, and the Quantico Injured Military Sportsmen Association. He has served as the rector of the Board of Trustees of the University of Richmond and chairman of the Board of Trustees of the Virginia Historical Society. We met in his West End office.

After high school, I went to the University of New Hampshire for six months. The dean of students told me he did not think I was very serious about school. I needed tightening up, so I enlisted in the Marine Corps, which was one of the best decisions I made in my life, and went to Parris Island.

I received a promotion out of Parris Island and went to advanced infantry training. Then I went to Sea School, and I served with the Marine detachment on the USS *Saratoga* (CVA-60), and spent the balance of my enlistment in the Mediterranean. They transferred me to Admiral Anderson's staff on the *Saratoga*, where I had some interesting experiences and spent time in Europe for the first time in my life. When I got out of the Marine Corps, I was a much more serious young man.

Your father, a World War II hero, must have liked that.

My father was very pleased when I finished Parris Island, as he had served side by side in combat with the Marines in the Pacific in World War II.

My father had two engineering degrees, one from VMI and the other from Cornell, and heavy construction experience. He was too old to be drafted but he volunteered, and the Navy formed the 71st Seabees Battalion around him and shipped him off to the Pacific. He was involved in constructing, under fire, the fighter fields at Okinawa, Bougainville and Guadalcanal. For these critical missions, he was awarded three Bronze Stars, all with "V"s for valor, a Legion of Merit, and several unit citations. He ended the war as a full captain in the Navy and was offered the job of admiral in charge of all Seabees worldwide. He said "Heck, no, I want to go home." So you can see, as a feckless youth, I was swimming upstream in his eyes.

During the summer of 1962, I graduated from the E. Claiborne Robins School of Business at the University of Richmond. I received several job offers in Dallas and New York, but I did not want to work in New York. I had an interesting offer from Henry Frost Oil Properties, a small exploration and drilling business in Dallas, Texas. The company was a wildcat driller for very wealthy individuals.

Mr. Frost was a wonderful gentleman who needed someone to whom he could delegate minor matters as he focused on the larger picture. I agreed, and Jane and I moved to Dallas. It was a great experience and a good place to mature, get away from Richmond, and learn about another business. The oil business was fascinating, and Mr. Frost gave me a lot of responsibility, which I appreciated.

Any notable memories of your early career in Dallas?

When I was in Dallas, I saw JFK only minutes before he was assassinated. Mr. Frost's offices were in the Davis Building on the thirteenth floor. Back in those days you could open the windows in these big old office buildings. My friends came over because the office was on the parade route and about ten blocks before Dealey Plaza. We were leaning out of the window of the Davis Building, looking at the procession going by. I remember it vividly.

Shortly thereafter, we were walking to the Petroleum Club for lunch and saw police cars recklessly speeding towards Dealey Plaza, in a very crowded downtown Dallas. We knew something was terribly wrong.

The town closed down. We never ate lunch, and I walked over to Merrill Lynch and watched the stock market take a nosedive. I went home. We had two young children, and we just stayed glued to the television. It was like being in a cave. It was just awful. The people of Dallas felt very, very guilty. I will never forget the feeling of remorse and guilt in that wonderful town.

Jane's father died in May of 1965. He was one of the owners of the local newspapers. Also, Mr. Frost was ill with an inner ear problem and was considering winding down his business. It was an appropriate time to transition back to Richmond, so I interviewed with local brokerage firms, as I knew I wanted to be in the financial business.

I received several offers and accepted the job with Wheat. For a short time I worked directly for Jim Wheat. One particular northern institution in Boston would hire me to do research projects that they did not want the big boys in New York to know about. Also, my individual client base grew.

At the time, Wheat was buying all of their national research from C. J. Lawrence. All of Wheat's internal research was focused primarily on local companies. Therefore, I needed national research for the larger accounts that I managed.

Jim Lowe was the director of research at C. J. Lawrence, so I sought his help. We did well together. We bought good names and made money for my clients. I was impressed with C. J. Lawrence, a really great boutique research firm.

The idea of investment counseling, where you were totally independent of any conflicts of interest, really appealed to me and to Jim Lowe. In 1970, I asked Jim if he would like to move to Richmond and start an investment management firm. He talked to his wife, Kay, and said yes to being my partner. Initially we only had enough money under management to pay the rent, hire a secretary, and buy some furniture. From that point, we grew steadily.

Our initial investment was $20,000, but soon we took out $7,000 each, so you could say the capitalization of the business was $6,000. Jim was a fabulous partner and a very smart analyst. He was the intellectual and I was the salesman. We both loved investing, the markets, and trying to figure out how to make money for our clients.

Tell me about the culture of Lowe, Brockenbrough.

You ask about the culture of our firm, which I am happy to discuss. Recently my son reminded me that a famous business guru once said that culture eats strategy for breakfast. We are serving families through four generations. The focus of our firm's associates is to do what is best for our clients in every single regard. It makes things straightforward when that is the mission, and you can build around that focus. Our firm is much like a well-functioning, happy family. Almost every day someone at the firm tells me what a great place this is to work, and that the culture is second to none.

Our firm continues to grow, so to enhance and protect our wonderful culture, we are very deliberate in our hiring of new associates. Our practice is to have a very detailed job description and to have many thorough interviews with the potential associate. Everyone in the firm has the opportunity to participate in this interview process. After we have firmwide consensus, the candidate goes to Psychological Consultants to be tested against the job description. If they pass with flying colors, we then have a new associate who can celebrate our culture.

Over the last five years, we have perpetuated our management to the next generation of young leaders with another group of accomplished thirty year olds, ready to follow today's team.

How did Lowe, Brockenbrough do during down markets of the last thirty years?

The 1987 correction was a surprise, but we did well because we did not panic. The bear market after 2000 was different. At the beginning our performance was outstanding, and then the high quality stocks got hit.

We learned a valuable lesson that we needed to better communicate, particularly in periods of market and economic stress.

That lesson helped us in 2006, 2007 and 2008, as we did a good job of protecting capital, getting out early, selling the bank stocks before they crashed, and telling our clients what we were doing, why we were doing it, and what concerned us.

At the bottom of the bear market, even though our clients were fearful, we began to put money back to work. We had built good reserves. We held good stocks. We protected well. We communicated vigorously with our clients about the markets and the economy and were rewarded because of our robust communication with our clients.

You have clients nationwide and a reputation as one of the preeminent firms in the business. You must receive buyout offers all the time.

Our firm has stated that it is not for sale because a larger acquiring firm would cut expenses and lay off employees to enhance their return on investment. Therefore, our partners and associates would lose, and our clients would receive reduced services and inferior performance. All lose in a sale, and the company would lose its culture. Therefore, we have determined to remain independent. There are very few independent firms remaining that were established at the time our firm was founded.

Please tell me about some of the prominent business leaders you've known in town.

I think Henry Lee Valentine is one of the most exceptional men in Richmond. When the courts would not allow the city to have elections, Henry remained on the City Council for years. I think he is a phenomenal gentleman with total integrity, and he is also a great leader.

I admire Buford Scott, a wonderful man and great citizen with a good financial mind. Just a great, great person. Caring and kind to the core.

I worked for Jim Wheat directly, and I like to tell Jim Wheat stories. He was a very exceptional man. He had an incredible mind and was as competitive as anybody I have ever known in my life. Carlyle Tiller, also of Wheat, First Securities, was a good investor.

During the summers when in Richmond, I worked at Branch, Cabell chalking boards. Mason New, a wonderful man, hired me. I had a great fondness for him.

Some years ago, I participated in an investment in AMF Bakery Equipment. Our CEO, Ken Newsome, reorganized and grew the company. We sold the company to Markel Ventures, and it became their first non-insurance acquisition. Through that transaction I came to know Markel Insurance, Steve Markel, and Tom Gayner. I have enormous respect for Steve Markel as a splendid person and believe he is one of the brightest people with whom I have ever worked. Tom Gayner is a gentleman: very smart, funny, and a first-rate investor.

What are some of your most memorable days?

There were important days in my adult life: marrying Jane, the birth of my children, entering the Marine Corps, and starting the business with Jim Lowe.

What is your outlook? Are you optimistic?

That is a great question. I think the stock market is fully valued, so we are cautious, but we have a positive outlook on the economy here in late 2017. The business community feels positive about the pro-business administration. There is the likelihood of a meaningful tax cut, which could result in two or three trillion dollars brought back to this country and reinvested in dividends, buybacks, infrastructure, new plants, and new employees. No one fully understands the impact this could have on the economy. It could be substantial.

The other is deregulation, as the administration is taking it on with a meat cleaver. Every week they are cutting more and more regulations. That has a profoundly positive influence on the cost structure of doing business, which in turn removes uncertainty. Some of the regulations were so ambiguous and difficult to interpret that it stifled investment.

What gives me great joy is when people I respect say, "Austin, I think you have built one of the finest teams of young people in the city of Richmond." I want to do a little jig. I try to refrain from doing that, but it fills me with pride. And the thing is, they are right. We have a group of exceptional people that work together beautifully.

ALVIN H. MILLER, JR.

A University of Richmond alumnus, Al's timing is good: he started his career on Main Street in August 1982, just as one of the greatest bull markets in history took off. I hope he never retires (why take the chance?). Al helped found James River Asset Management, a registered investment advisory firm, in 1995. Other investment professionals are known to pay him the ultimate compliment: they ask him for retirement planning advice.

I'd always had a real interest in the stock market. I bought my first stock at twelve and held it until it ultimately went bankrupt—General Motors. After college I worked for a savings and loan then took a sales job, to gain the sales experience I'd need to enter the brokerage industry. I did so in August of '82, when a fellow I knew socially, Clyde Pitchford, helped me get an interview with the manager at Dean Witter.

How have clients changed over the years?

Clients are more knowledgeable today and more aware of what's happening in the markets. There are 24/7 news channels and dedicated outlets like Bloomberg and CNBC that deliver information instantaneously. The days when the broker was almost like a priest, sort of the gatekeeper of Wall Street information, ended a long time ago.

When I started in the business, the branch manager would walk around the office, complaining that it cost him a thousand dollars a month to put a quote machine on our desks, and that we needed to produce business to pay for it. The quote machine was a piece of proprietary, clunky hardware connected by a big, fat high-speed telephone line to an office in New York where the news and stock quotes and account information were all disseminated. It did cost quite a bit of money. Nowadays, anybody with a cell phone has access to ten times as much information, faster and more accurate. So that's really changed the dynamic between the broker and the clients.

One of the brokers in that office, Bill Longan, was farsighted. He'd say that one day these things we call PCs would be so small and so cheap they'd fall out of cereal boxes. He was directionally very much on the money.

Has more information led to better stock market performance?

Probably not. Number one, there's a tidal wave of information. What's the old analogy? Trying to drink out of a fire hose? But it still takes an awful lot of time to corral that information, organize it, make sense of it, and put it in some sort of useful decision-making format. And it takes some degree of knowledge and insight to sort out what's really important from the day-to-day noise. So unless clients are really dedicated to spending several hours a day studying and following the markets and educating themselves, they're really not that much better prepared to make decisions. That's where the experience and deeper knowledge set of a registered rep makes a difference.

Number two, investor psychology hasn't changed a bit, and customers make the same mistakes. So do brokers; so do money managers. It all still comes down to fear and greed. Look at Bitcoin.

But I would say that clients, even though they're subject to the same emotional pulls, are better informed today. You can have a higher-level conversation with most of them today than maybe you could have had thirty years ago, when you called them up on the phone and said, hey, let's buy Philip Morris. Almost all of our clients now go through a pretty extensive planning process, something we never emphasized back in the day. We focus on asset allocation, risk tolerance, income needs, time horizon, and so forth.

Registered investment advisors eliminate a lot of the classic conflicts of interest, and I think it puts clients at ease when they understand that we're not emotionally wrapped up in one transaction over another, and that our recommendations come from a fiduciary basis. A registered investment advisor is a fiduciary and required to act in the client's best interest, not merely recommend something that's just suitable for a client. So that has made a tremendous difference, from the client's side of things, and frankly from ours as well.

From our point of view, it's been a get-rich-slowly business, building clients and growing their assets. Quite a few of our clients are going on twenty, twenty-five years with us.

III

STOCKBROKERS AND TRADERS

WILLIE WALTERS

Willie, former head trader at Branch, Cabell, and his wife Lizz run Walters and Company, a real estate investment, property management, brokerage, and investment firm in Denver.

I spent most of my career at Branch, Cabell, as a market maker and then as an institutional sales trader. I started in September of 1982, and I left in July of 1998.

In the spring of '82, the Dow Jones was trading around the high seven hundreds, low eight hundreds, but the market took off in August. The Dow Jones was at 942 the day I started, in mid-September. Trading desks were getting very busy and employed what I referred to as *warm body hires.* They just needed people to answer the phones.

William Wilkerson, head of trading at Branch, Cabell, was dating my sister at the time, which is how I came into the business. I was hired as a gopher, literally sitting at a tiny little desk that was probably two feet by four feet, in a corner with a telephone and a set of Pink Sheets.[11] My job was to get quotes. If a stock wasn't on Nasdaq, and a lot of over-the-counter stocks weren't back then, you had to call around and get quotes. The rule was that you had to get at least three quotes. I wanted to be an overachiever, so I'd get five. I wasn't allowed to execute the orders; I got the quotes and somebody else would execute the order.

Another part of my job was to get lunch or coffee for anybody on the desk. After a few months of that, I was allowed to execute Pink Sheet orders, and within six months I was given a list of stocks to trade, one of which was the RF&P,[12] a $250 stock with an enormous spread.

I was a Nasdaq trader throughout the eighties. Jimmy White and I then started the institutional business at Branch, Cabell in 1989. When

William Wilkerson left in 1989, I became head of the over-the-counter desk.

I learned things the hard way. Early on, a guy named Pat McCloskey, head trader for Wellington Management, called our trading desk. I took the call, and he said, "I'm Pat McCloskey, and I want to buy fifty thousand shares of XYZ." At the time, I didn't know anything about institutional trading. I was a market maker. I told him that I was only good for a thousand shares, and that I would make a call. He laughed and asked if I knew who he was. I told him I didn't give a **** who he was.

That was my baptism by fire as to how institutional business worked. As a firm, we realized that we probably needed to tighten some stuff up, so we hired Jimmy White. When I look back, Jimmy White taught me so much about so many things. Jimmy and his brother Stafford were instrumental in my wife and me meeting. They introduced us.

Jimmy was very good with people and very fun to be around. He had a certain edge to him that would come out every now and again. Not too many people saw it, unless you worked directly with him. He also brought structure to everything. To this day I still keep a legal pad next to me and write down all my calls and discussions and notes, dating every page—a trait I picked up from Jimmy.

He taught me the value of consistently calling institutions and giving updates, and that delivering bad news was more important than delivering good news.

We did a ton of business with Friess Associates, a big account, and Duncan Hurst, a West Coast account. We would do business with T. Rowe Price, and a huge amount of business with Safeco back in the day.

There were a lot of great ideas pitched by smart brokers at Branch, Cabell. Any examples that you can remember?

Hunter Thompson was a retail broker with incredible stock ideas. He would call institutions off the cuff, and because his ideas were so good, they listened. At one point he was big on a computer storage company, EMC. What could you possibly need storage for? It was a dollar stock at the time. We placed millions of shares of that stuff institutionally.[13]

Micros Systems was another one. People just didn't get the significance of point-of-sale cash registers. That stock was a pig, and it traded like mud. But Hunter got it.[14] Now you can't go into a restaurant, bar, or hotel without seeing Micros or some copycat.

Hunter had an uncanny eye for talent. One example: Ted Goins was a waiter at the Country Club of Virginia. Hunter talked to him and thought, this kid is pretty bright. He brought Goins in and made him an analyst.

Ted came up with an idea: Wiland Services, a catalog company. It was a penny stock, and he convinced people to buy it at ten cents, fifteen cents, twenty cents, thirty cents. In 1992, two years later, it was LBOd at six dollars and change plus one share of the new company, Concepts Direct, initially trading at fifty-two cents a share. So if you bought Wiland at ten cents and held it for the whole ride, you got six and a quarter dollars in cash and a share of stock that eventually topped twenty in 1996. It was the longest home run ball that I've ever heard of. We put away a ton of it. And this kid, a former waiter at CCV, dug it up.

Ascend Communications was big.[15] We were the first firm in the country to write that up. People just didn't get it when it came to telecom and technology. People couldn't grasp how much and how quickly tech was changing the world. Telebit, you know, their technology is irrelevant now, but in the transition from analog to digital, it filled a niche. And in all fairness, there were some dogs in there too. As always.

Our retail client base was heavily invested in regional companies. We did a pretty good job in some of them, such as Wampler Longacre (WLR Foods[16]). Our Harrisonburg office knew all the turkey farmers and knew where all the bodies were buried. We also knew the furniture makers out in the western part of the state pretty well.

Not all regional stocks worked out. An example was Salem Carpet Mills. One day, our analyst came into the research meeting and said, "Salem Carpet's earnings are due out in two weeks. They're not returning my calls. I'm smelling a rat here. I think everybody needs to sell Salem Carpet."

Every broker in the system had their customers sell Salem Carpet. This was back in the day of a half a point markdown in commissions, and as a trader, I was picking up the spread because somehow there were buyers everywhere for this stock. Three days later Salem Carpet was bought out for a 42 percent premium. Oops.

The market was flying in 1987. I was twenty-four years old and doing pretty well for myself. I bought my first house and first brand-new car, a 1987 Chrysler LeBaron. I was pretty full of myself. My personal license plate was "4N8TH."

Around that time, after work, I was walking down Cary Street to Sam Miller's with William Wilkerson, Jimmy Thomas,[17] and Ken Palmer.[18] I pointed out my new car, and asked what they thought. They wanted to know what the license plate meant. I told them, I'll trade anything *for an eighth*. They were disgusted that I would show my hand. "You're going to ruin this business if you tell people how skinny you'll trade stuff." Trading something for an eighth at that time was considered trading it skinny. Now, beating the spread by $0.0001 is touted.

Traders worked hard and played hard.

Trader conventions were basically a big drunk. But you would really get to know your colleagues. For the most part, we were all friendly competitors. That's how you'd build the relationships. It was the beginning of the end when that type of relationship building started to go away, in my opinion. We represented clients. We knew who the bad guys were (like the wholesalers). I shouldn't say they were bad guys, but they just had a different set of priorities. The Sherwoods, where I eventually worked, the Troster-Singers, the Herzogs, Mayer and Schweitzer. They were considered fast money guys.

Back in the day, Nasdaq stocks traded with spreads. The higher the price, the more illiquid the stock, the bigger the spread. Those spreads existed because of the risk involved. When we made market quotes, they were firm. They weren't bull****. RF&P traded with a hundred-dollar spread because it was really illiquid. So if I quoted you a hundred-dollar bid, I'm going to buy it from you at a hundred. And if it's offered at 150, I'm going to sell it to you at 150. The spread gave us the time to find the other side of the trade. The more illiquid the stock, the wider the spread. On the other hand, an actively traded, highly liquid stock like a Microsoft would trade with an eighth of a point spread.

Electronic trading changed everything. SOES trading[19] was rolled out after the crash in '87 because market makers weren't answering their phones. Instinet and SOES marked the beginning of electronic trading, high-frequency trading. Characters popped up to take advantage of the new system. Harvey Houtkin was probably one of the better-known *SOES bandits*.

SOES abuse was simply entering order after order after order. Houtkin had his traders enter orders over and over and over again into the SOES system. That was essentially the beginning of high-frequency trading. In the meantime, a real seller would come in over the phone and say, "Hey this is Lehman Brothers. We have XYZ for sale." And I'd have to give "SOES ahead" (i.e., Houtkin's multiple orders). That disadvantaged prices for real customers. So to combat that, a certain degree of collusion, for lack of a better word, arose between the market makers, the guys that we'd see out on the road. They had to defend themselves from the SOES bandits.

Then Shelly Maschler came in and took it a step further. He was with First Jersey originally, and later started Datek Securities. Shelly started making markets in sixteenths, which had never been done before. His quotes were only good for one hundred shares. You'd be trying to work a trade and he'd game the system and break up your trade. Clients lost; market makers lost; no one won but him. That was the evolution of electronic trading.

Later, Shelly went from sixteenths to thirty-seconds, just to piss off the establishment and break up trades. The joke then went around that somebody broke in his office and stabbed him. But he was okay because the knife only went in a thirty-second of an inch. Regulators eventually banned Shelly from the business.

In October 1987, Kendall Avery started, for lack of a better term, as my assistant. I had to teach him the language. I also had to teach him who to trust and who not to trust. And the quintessential guy not to trust was Shelly. We called Shelly, to introduce Kendall. Of course traders are a very colorful bunch, language-wise. "Hey Shelly, how you doin'?" He answers, "Hey quote boy, how *you* doin'?" When I told him I had a new guy on the other line, Shelly says, "Hey, quote boy junior, how you doin'? I need some business. You got to send me some orders. I got to put more wood on my station wagon." We hung up, laughing at what a tool bag that guy was.

The trading community was pretty close. It was very collegial all over the country. We were genuinely friends. Relationships were built on trust. As the regulatory environment changed, trust eroded. Without the ability to make a personal connection, how can you trust somebody? Or be trusted, for that matter. That was an evolution, and part of what drove me out of the business eventually.

I was a slow learner. It took me another twelve years to hang up the cleats. It's kind of sad, because it was a great business. The vast majority of people in the business truly believed they were doing good. We weren't driven by greed (some were, though). We were driven by a genuine desire to do the best we could for our client.

Branch, Cabell was one of the last of the old-line family firms.

The managing partner when I started was Mason New. He had bought controlling interest in the firm from the Cabell family in the 1950s. He was in his seventies and smoked like a chimney. He sat there and he traded off of the tape, but used to call down for quotes if he missed a stock on the tape.

And guess who he would call? Me. He'd want a quote on something, even though he'd sit there with a quote machine right in front of him, which he used primarily as an ashtray.

One day when I was busy with something, I got frustrated with Mr. New and told him to punch the quote up on the Bunker Ramo right in front of him. "I don't know how to work this damn thing, boy." I told him that I'd come up and show him, but I wasn't very polite.

I showed him how it worked. That was the beginning of a friendship that was very important to me. I can't begin to tell you what a genius this guy was, and the wealth of knowledge and experience in that man's head. I had enormous respect for him.

He told me that I had to remember that I was dealing with people's money, and that's second only to their family in terms of their importance. And for some people, it's actually number one. So I had to treat that responsibility with respect. That's what I was taught, but I think that's changed a bit since. The primary focus was the client, and if you took care of the client, they would take care of you. That was it. Plain and simple, nothing fancy. ◼

Chairman of the Board and co-founder of Thompson Davis & Co., Hunter has a decades-long reputation as one of the best small-cap stock pickers on Main Street. His analysis, supported by a wide array of contacts in the industries he covers, focuses on sales and earnings growth and market sentiment. A lifelong resident of Richmond, Hunter is a graduate of St. Christopher's School, Washington and Lee University, and the Darden School of Business at the University of Virginia.

My father used to buy my brother Matt and me five or ten shares of stock for Christmas back in the '40s and the early '50s, which is how we developed a fascination for stocks. I'm not sure what Matt did with his shares, but I sold my shares of all those great companies like Standard Oil of New Jersey and the Life Insurance Company of Virginia when I began at the Darden School. A friend at business school at the time, in 1961 or 1962 when the market was hot, dealt with a broker in Roanoke, at the firm of Francis I. duPont, who would get us shares of hot initial public offerings.

Classmates and friends of mine (such as Carter Fox, who later ran Chesapeake Corporation) and I would go down to a local brokerage after class and watch the tape. We were sitting there one afternoon and saw the ticker symbol "ALB" continuously go by, up ten bucks every trade. "ALB" was Albemarle Paper, and they'd recently bought out Ethyl Corporation. We watched the stock move from forty to fifty to over one hundred in an afternoon. You get interested when you see stocks move like that.

We were also in the board room during the Cuban Missile Crisis, when the market was down and the tape was running late. We saw big stocks like Zenith go by, down five dollars, ten dollars, and more.

I think it was my need for action that attracted me to the stock market. After business school, I worked for Prudential in Boston. My job was to travel around New England and find companies that wanted to borrow money from Prudential. They wanted to loan five million dollars a day. I found out later that it was Prudential who financed Albemarle's takeover of Ethyl. Mr. Gottwald borrowed all that money from Pru and another big insurance company.

I became frustrated after a few years at Prudential. Here I was, knocking on doors and trying to lend money to people who had the kind of jobs I wanted—entrepreneurs, young guys, mostly, who had built businesses and who were doing something productive.

I came back to Richmond for vacation around that time. A friend of mine from W&L, a lawyer in Richmond, told me that the Clover Room was for sale. The Clover Room was run by a guy named Beattie Luck, a friend of my parents. It was so successful. He made his own ice cream, chicken salad, shrimp salad, ham salad, and limeades. Beattie was always there to shake your hand when you came in.

I immediately told Beattie that I'd like to buy the Clover Room. He wanted eighty thousand dollars for it. So I left a perfectly fantastic job with my own office, secretary, and parking place in the Prudential Center in Boston to come down here and run Thompson's Family Restaurant.

Fortunately, before going to Darden, I had worked for B. B. Munford and Henry Valentine at Davenport one summer as a board boy. After my restaurant went under—which didn't take very long, to tell you the truth (maybe a year)—Davenport hired me to do basically what I'd been doing at Prudential, which was to find people who needed capital, essentially an investment banking function.

After six months of knocking on doors, Henry Valentine commented that I'd been working really hard, developed a Rolodex with about 150 names in it, but had closed only one deal, which earned the firm $1,250. He said I should get registered as a stockbroker, which I did. Pretty soon, I was making three thousand dollars a month.

A year later I was making $150 a month, however. I knew Mason New at Branch, Cabell, who had just come over from IBM to work for his father. I joined Branch, Cabell, where they offered me a thousand dollars a month, which was a hell of an enticement. I became director of research at Branch, Cabell within ten or so years, because I was able to find good stocks that went up, and built a good customer book.

A highlight of that time involved a company called Pulsecom, a company in Northern Virginia that Ferris & Co. brought public in the early '70s, at five dollars a share. Pulsecom was run by George Pierce, an individual who'd attended St. Christopher's and had been voted the person most likely to succeed. He went on to MIT. He was a genius.

The market collapsed, and Pulsecom fell to two dollars. I knew the company and its business really well from my days knocking on doors for

Davenport. I put all my clients into the stock. Pulsecom was bought out for sixteen dollars a share a year or so later.

Little things like that through the years kept my interest very, very high. The market collapsed in January 1973, and the rest of the '70s were terrible for many stocks. I still made money for my clients, though, because I found stocks that had reasons to go up.

The communications industry was undergoing great change. AT&T was broken up. Western Electric lost its monopoly. Ted Turner started cable, CNN, using satellites. We became involved with companies that made the components to receive satellite signals. Through the decades, I've been lucky to have been exposed to lots of changes in the way the world worked, and to have benefited from that knowledge. That's why I'm still working, because it's in my blood.

Are you still active in the market every day?

Absolutely. You ought to see the market today [the DJIA was up 250 points at that moment – *Ed*.]. BlackRock is up twelve dollars. Cigna's up almost six. Berkshire Hathaway is up four. Boeing is up another twelve. It's crazy. UnitedHealth is at a new high, up five dollars. It's just incredible what Trump has done to inspire confidence in the U.S. and the economy.

Are you short any stocks?

No. But I shorted one stock one time, Sykes Datatronics. It's a good story.

I first heard about Sykes Datatronics from the former head of Pulsecom, who moved to Sarasota and set up a company that manufactured telephone equipment. One of Sykes' components measured usage and effectiveness of incoming and outgoing phone calls for companies, to increase productivity. The stock was selling for about five bucks a share at the time.

Mason New and I visited Sykes in Rochester. The CEO was Hollywood material, with charisma, and a bachelor's of science in engineering at Yale University. We looked at the log-in books in the reception area, and representatives from all the Bell Telephone companies had been signing in. All of them were buying product from Sykes, so we knew we were onto something. The stock went to twelve, and finally reached 100-plus, before splitting three-for-one.

Jack Muldowney of
Scott & Stringfellow,
August 1988.

Entrance to the
Mutual Building, one
of Richmond's first
high rise buildings,
909 East Main Street.

Belcher's Barber Shop in June 1988, an institution in the Mutual Building basement. Opened by Dalton William Belcher in 1967.

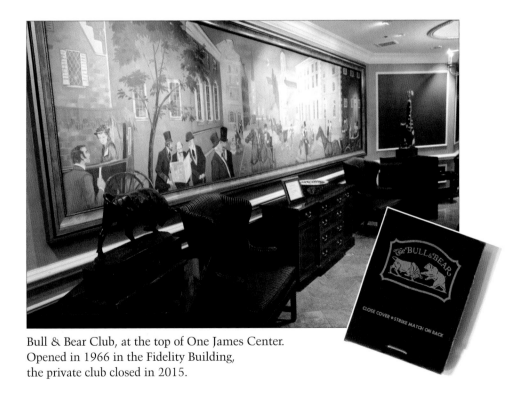

Bull & Bear Club, at the top of One James Center. Opened in 1966 in the Fidelity Building, the private club closed in 2015.

Anderson, Strudwick to Form New Investment Banking Firm

Edward C. Anderson and Edmund Strudwick, Jr., both formerly connected with Scott & Stringfellow, will form an investment banking firm under the name of Anderson, Strudwick & Co., with offices at 807 East Main St.

Mr. Anderson said the new firm will open for business January 15. It will engage in the underwriting and distribution of stocks, bonds

been office manager since 1942. Mr. Muldowney, with the firm since 1929, is also secretary and treasurer of the Richmond Stock Exchange.

Other partners in the firm include Buford Scott, Walter S. Robertson, James H. Scott, Marion N. Fitzgerald and Thomas D. Neal.

WIDE EXPERIENCE

RICHMOND NEWS LEADER

January 2, 1948

Edward Anderson and Edmund Strudwick left Scott & Stringfellow in 1948 to form Anderson, Strudwick & Co.

Fidelity Bankers Life Building, Ninth and Main Streets, late 1980.

THE WALL STREET JOURNAL, Thursday, March 5, 1970

This announcement is neither an offer to sell nor a solicitation of an offer to buy any of these securities. The offering is made only by the Prospectus.

New Issue   March 4, 1970

175,000 Shares

BEST PRODUCTS CO., INC.

Common Stock
($1.00 Par Value)

Price $10.00 per Share

Copies of the Prospectus may be obtained in any State in which this announcement is circulated from only such of the undersigned or other dealers or brokers as may lawfully offer these securities in such State.

Wheat & Co., Inc.

Anderson & Strudwick   Branch, Cabell & Co.

Craigie Incorporated   Davenport & Co.

Ferris & Company   Interstate Securities Corporation

Investment Corporation of Virginia Affiliate

Mackall & Coe   Mason & Company, Incorporated

Mason-Hagan, Inc.   Scott & Stringfellow

The Cecil-Waller Company

Kaufman Bros. Co.   Lane, Sterling & Company, Inc.

Mason & Lee, Inc.   Strader & Company, Incorporated

Wyllie and Thornhill, Inc.

Best Products 1970 Initial Public Offering tombstone, managed by Wheat & Co. Of 18 underwriters, only the Scott & Stringfellow and Davenport names survive.

Best Products Inc. Is Expected to Seek Chapter 11 Protection From Creditors

By GEORGE ANDERS
Staff Reporter of THE WALL STREET JOURNAL

Best Products Inc. will file for Chapter 11 bankruptcy-law protection from creditors today, according to executives close to the retailer.

Best's decision puts it on a growing list of U.S. retailers that have been financially squeezed after taking on big debts in the late 1980s. In the past 18 months, heavily indebted retailers such as Federated Department Stores Corp., Allied Stores Corp., Garfinckel's Inc. and others have also payments to trade creditors can continue.

Best appears to be betting that its abrupt move into Chapter 11 will preserve more of the company's underlying value than if the retailer had tried to continue operating partly stocked stores this year. Best and Adler & Shaykin had tried for about a month to negotiate an out-of-bankruptcy debt restructuring, but with little luck. In a letter to suppliers last week, Best President Stewart Kasen had characterized those talks as "difficult and tenu-

THE WALL STREET JOURNAL.

January 5, 1991

Best Products' first bankruptcy filing, 1991. It filed for bankruptcy a second and final time in 1996.

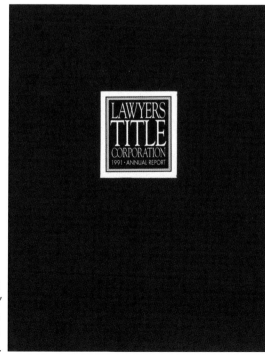

Lawyers Title 1991 annual shareholders' report, its first after the spin-off from Universal Leaf Tobacco Co.

First National Bank Building, Ninth and Main Streets.
Built in 1912 and later a home to First & Merchants
and Craigie, it's now an apartment building.

Richmond Society of Financial Analysts invitation to its
lunch meeting, held September 11, 2001. Bill Johnston,
president of the NYSE, was scheduled to speak.

The Richmond Society of Financial Analysts

cordially invites you to attend

a speech given by

Mr. William R. Johnston

President, New York Stock Exchange

Tuesday, September 11, 2001

at four-thirty

The Commonwealth Club

Richmond, Virginia

R.s.v.p. by September 7
Louis O. Bowman (804) 644-1128

THE WALL STREET JOURNAL.

SATURDAY, MAY 23, 2015

Lessons From a Buffett Believer

Earlier this month, a crowd filled an auditorium to attend a corporate annual meeting at which a folksy investor spoke about his company and the secrets of success. But they weren't in Omaha to hear Warren Buffett talking about Berkshire Hathaway; this crowd came to

THE INTELLIGENT INVESTOR
JASON ZWEIG

the Altria Theater in Richmond, Va., for the annual meeting of Markel Corp.

One of the speakers, Thomas Gayner, co-president and chief investment officer of the financial-holding company, has an outstanding record as a portfolio manager. He works only for Markel and doesn't take outside clients, but every investor can learn from him.

Over the past 15 years, Mr. Gayner's stocks have returned an average of 11.3% annually, while the S&P 500 index of big U.S. stocks has returned 4.2%, counting dividends. Last year, when winning portfolio managers were scarcer than vegetarians at a pig roast, Mr. Gayner outperformed the S&P 500 by 4.9 percentage points. His portfolio fell 34% in the market rout of 2008, but that was better than the S&P 500's 37% loss.

You never would know any of this from listening to Mr. Gayner. After a good year, most portfolio managers beat their chests even harder than they beat the market; Mr. Gayner's 2014 report merely said, "our overall equity portfolio earned 18.6%," without even mentioning that the S&P 500 was up 13.7%.

Several of Mr. Gayner's peers describe him as a good investor who has become great by keeping he is but

good. He is no Warren Buffett, and he is keenly aware of his limitations. "I tell investors, 'You're smarter than I am, but I'm managing your money,'" Mr. Gayner says. "'If you see me doing something I shouldn't be, tell me.'"

But he also makes the most of his strengths.

Markel's costs are so low that he can

manage its $4.5 billion stock portfolio for less than 0.01% in annual expenses, about one-70th the cost of the average U.S. stock mutual fund.

Mr. Gayner, 53 years old, worked as an accountant, a stockbroker and an equity analyst before joining Markel in 1990. He looks for profitable businesses with

Pretty good company: Tom Gayner, with Warren Buffett and Charlie Munger.

Walter Anderson,
broker at Scott &
Stringfellow, 1982.

Ninth and Main Streets,
looking south.

A client of mine (still one of my best clients after thirty or forty years) who was with Pulsecom called me later and told me the Sykes products weren't working. They were blowing up and catching fire. The Bell companies were sending them back.

I called Robert Wilson, the short seller who was a client of a friend of mine, and gave him the story. He began shorting the stock. By the time it was all over, he sent me a check for forty-three thousand dollars for the research (which I had to give to Tony Frank).[20]

Wall Street analysts then came back and re-recommended the stock because of the halo effect of its leader. They ran the stock back to sixteen. Wilson shorted it again, and it went back to six. I was in Nags Head, and Wilson called and left a message for me: "I love you. Bob Wilson."

Why did you start Thompson Davis?

First, Tucker Anthony bought Branch, Cabell in 2000. When they made us an offer we were all ears, and sold to them. RBC[21] then bought Tucker Anthony in 2001.

I had formed a group at Branch, Cabell called the EHT Group, which conducted research and institutional sales, and managed money on a discretionary basis. Bill Davis was with me. Some people from RBC visited us at the time of the acquisition and told us that while they liked what we were doing, we couldn't do it under the RBC name. They already had an institutional research and sales department. They said they'd do anything to help us, but we couldn't work for them.

So the EHT Group moved up to the sixteenth floor and RBC provided us with back office services, a really sweet deal. That's how Thompson Davis started.

Another highlight occurred when Paul Edmunds, who later left to start his own hedge fund, discovered a company called OmniVision, based in Silicon Valley, in 2002 or 2003. The company made chips for mobile phone cameras. OmniVision was trading around ten dollars a share. Gene McCown, the CFO, was on a road show to make presentations to money managers, and he visited Paul in his office. Paul invited me to sit in. Mr. McCown told us about the company's operations, who they were selling to, and what their strategy was.

We bought the stock, and it began to move higher. In the meantime, OmniVision caught the attention of Citron Research, a short selling firm. Firms like Citron made money by finding out what investors were short what stocks, and then writing research reports that recommended shorting that particular stock. They would sell the bogus reports to those short sellers, to broadcast the idea and push the stock lower. Questionable activity, in my opinion. Other firms that promoted short ideas became involved also.

We thought the shorts' involvement was great, because we knew we were right and they were wrong, and it gave us an opportunity to make money. I would call Mr. McCown at 7:30 or so at night, which was 4:30 p.m. his time, before I went home. He'd be very frank. He would never give us anything that he shouldn't have given us, but just confirmed what we knew.

We loaded the boat with OmniVision. The company reported a great quarter. Then another great quarter. The shorts had to cover, and drove the stock to sixty. We made a lot of money on OmniVision.

Another stock story? One of my best friends from W&L and St. Christopher's and UVA, Darracott Vaughan, was one of the world's great urologists. He was highly regarded worldwide for his skill in treating prostate cancer. Darracott was down here for a St. Christopher's reunion, and we ended up at my house for an after-party drink, where he told us about a new robotic surgical system, *da Vinci*, made by a company called Intuitive Surgical.

Darracott wanted to buy the stock. He didn't need to use da Vinci himself but reasoned that younger surgeons would need it and use it. So we bought the stock for around twelve for all our clients. When it reached one hundred, Darracott sold his, so I sold all mine. Ultimately it went over four hundred dollars a share.

There were many other stories of great stock moves, but also many setbacks along the way. Usually, as with Sykes Datatronics, those occurred when company managements were less than forthcoming when their story changed. The worst setback occurred when I had a CFO on the phone. He said he'd call me back in a minute. The stock was then halted and an announcement was made that the company was being investigated for accounting irregularities. The stock never reopened.

Kendall is a vice-president with Oppenheimer & Co. Inc. and a proud Virginia Military Institute alumnus. Pictures of the Institute and his diploma decorate his office in the Williams Mullin Center, where I sat under his painting of "The Last Meeting" (of Stonewall Jackson and Robert E. Lee) for the interview.

I started in the business October 1, 1987, eighteen days before the Crash. I was in over-the-counter trading at Branch, Cabell. I had quit my job in sales at Dillard Paper Company, where I was making good money. I took a big cut in pay, and eighteen days later the market crashed. That was on a Monday. The volume that day was six hundred million shares. Blew every record away at that point. Six hundred million shares today is IBM.

We had to physically match up trades – buys and sells – that went to the New York Stock Exchange. There were so many orders that we had to go in the following Saturday to work on matching up these trades. William Wilkerson, the partner in charge, picked me up that morning. I lived on West Franklin Street; he lived on Monument Avenue. We were on the Downtown Expressway (I remember exactly where we were) and I said, "William, let me ask you a question. Do I still have a job?"

He replied, "Well, I'm not sure, because I'm not sure if *I* do." And he was a partner. That's not a good answer. That's not reassuring.

I worked on the trading desk with Willie Walters, William Wilkerson's brother-in-law. I heard Willie lost a half a million dollars of the firm's money on the day of the Crash, and William lost a million dollars. And Branch, Cabell was not a big firm.

On the day of the Crash, I was answering phones and calling market makers. It was bedlam. When I would call the trading desk of Bear Stearns, a large New York market maker, to hit one of the bids they posted, they'd just pick the phone up and hang up. They weren't standing by their bids. Stock prices were just collapsing. Nobody wanted to buy any stock. It was crazy.

The technological aspect of trading was just coming into practice, but for the most part the job involved typical day-to-day transactions all day long, talking to other market makers. You'd talk to people all over the country. It was really cool. That's where jokes came from. Jokes in the trading department made their way around the country instantaneously, through this network of traders. Invariably bad stuff happens, and somebody makes a joke about it. And immediately everybody's heard that joke about whatever. Really tasteless stuff. The *Challenger* blew up. We got jokes about that.

Back in the day when stocks traded with a quarter-point spread and somebody could make some money, traders would say, "I'll buy three thousand, and let me work that order." So it created stability in the markets. That's gone. And that's why you see these tremendous drops. There will be another flash crash, don't worry. Something will happen, and when the machines take over, there will be no human being to step in and say, "I'll buy that, let me work that order." It's just computers, algorithms. They have no emotions; they have no sense of what is a good buy, what is a bargain, of creating a market.

The disappearance of human traders in favor of automation was one of the worst things that ever happened. They say it's good for the consumer and for the investor. But there are always unintended consequences. We were down a thousand points during that flash crash. I was sitting here, we're down seventy-five points, and all of a sudden we're down seven hundred, eight hundred, nine hundred—bang, bang, bang.

And then the market came back. Nobody knows what caused it. There was a fat finger theory, that somebody typed the wrong button on a keyboard. Something's going to shock the market again, and it's going to knock it down so far and so fast people will wonder what in the world just happened.

Jack Muldowney, at Scott & Stringfellow, was a memorable trader. My first interaction with him was at a function at the old Bull & Bear Club. A guy named Pat Ryan, I believe, from Johnston, Lemon in Washington came down to speak. He spoke, and afterward this guy stood up and asked a longwinded, blowhard question. Being new in the business, I remember thinking the guy should just shut up. Muldowney stood up and interrupted him: "If you would shut up, we could get out of here a lot sooner," or something to that effect. He was an Irishman who didn't take anything from anybody.

After the Crash, I started to make markets. I was trading a couple of stocks, but volume dried up. The whole business shrunk, and Branch, Cabell went through layoffs. They laid off people in the back office. One of the people laid off was the order entry guy on the teletype machine, where orders went to our correspondent, Cowen and Company, to execute our trades on the floor of the New York Stock Exchange. When he was fired, I moved into the job.

By 1990, it was obvious things weren't improving. And I thought, you know what, I was in sales before. I've got my license. I'm going to go out and be a broker.

Who are some of the notable managers you've worked with?

Tony Frank, at Branch, Cabell, was one. For a young guy, he was a scary dude. He didn't suffer fools. He'd fire you in a heartbeat. I remember one trader, Mike, came in and said to Willie, "Where's William? I'm going tell him that I've told the SEC about securities violations in this department."

Willie brought Mike to William, who repeats: "I have contacted the SEC about potential security violations here." William said, "Let's go see Tony Frank." That was the last we saw of Mike. Tony fired him right there.

I interviewed with a couple of other firms in 1990. One guy I interviewed with was Mike Bannon, who is now my manager. He was bigger than life, I thought. I can remember him to this day telling me: "My job is to stir the pot here. These brokers, keep them going. My branch will do more this year than all of Branch, Cabell will do." I don't recall exactly, but I think he was with Smith Barney at the time.

And I interviewed with Ed Kienel at Dean Witter. Went back and interviewed with Jerry Green. Interviewed with Merrill Lynch. Interviewed with Don Whitley at Paine Webber.

At Branch, Cabell, let's see, who else was there? After the Crash, they invited a few more people to become partners because they needed the capital inflow. So Hank Miller, Cliff Singer, and Lee Graham became partners. I don't know if John Lucas was already a partner then. He was in charge of the bond department.

How did I get my customers? Cold calls. Back in those days, you could do it. It was in the middle of the savings and loan crisis. All of the local bank stocks looked like they were going to zero. I still remember one issue of Signet Bank bonds. They were 9⅝ coupon, due 2000, and they were non-callable. And they were trading at seventy-four, which gave them something like a 15 percent yield.

I got on the phone, and I went right down Cherokee Road. I had a reverse directory, and I called people. The beauty of that was you didn't have to try to talk about the ins and outs. It was Mr. Customer, we have some Signet Bank bonds. They're yielding 15 percent. Is that of interest to you? Yes or no was all I was looking for. I didn't want to have to explain it. I wanted the person who said, "Wow, Signet Bank." I wanted the person that understood immediately. And a lot of people knew immediately. I opened a lot of accounts with that Signet Bank bond. They were non-callable, and they traded back to par and matured. From there, you get referrals.

Back then, drinking went hand in hand with the business. After work, people would go down to The Tobacco Company or other bars. Not every day, but compared to today, it was a great time. Just a lot of fun. It was young people. And it's not a young business anymore. You look at this office, and I'm one of the youngest people in here, and I'm fifty-seven. We were a bunch of twenty-, thirty-, forty-year-olds. People making money, and it was fun.

There's a firm in town—you know them—Mann, Armistead & Epperson. Jimmy Mann had a seat at The Tobacco Company that had his name on it. I'm pretty sure it did. Probably still there.

Today, all firms are interested in is gathering assets. They want fee-based accounts because it's smooth business. It's recurring revenue as opposed to commission business, which is lumpy. The market gets bad and nobody trades.

The biggest stock I was involved in was Monster Energy. It was called Hanson Natural back then, and I bought it at four dollars a share, and I think I sold it at eight. And I was a genius. And then it went to two hundred and split. It went to two hundred again and split. I wanted to commit suicide every time I saw it.

I hate to say this but my biggest loser may have been CreditTrust.[22] I lost a lot of money on CreditTrust.

The hardest part of this business, at least in stock picking, is not what to buy, it's when to sell it. You just never know what a stock's going to do. Hope springs eternal, and you always want to think that it's going to one hundred. No matter what it is, they've got the greatest products since you name it, and it's going to be huge. And it does. The stock goes up, and the higher it goes, the more you believe that.

Then it starts going down. And you go, "Eh, it's just a pullback." And it might rally some, and you say, "Yeah, okay." Then it goes back down. It's just an emotional roller coaster. You shouldn't, but you want to think that it's still a good company and things are going well. But there's an old adage, and it's true: Management lies. ■

The Muldowney name is among the most respected on Main Street. Jack joined Scott & Stringfellow in 1970 and headed equity trading until his retirement in 2016. His father, Joe, started with Scott & Stringfellow as a board boy just months before the 1929 Crash and remained with the firm for almost fifty years. A Benedictine High School and University of Richmond graduate, Jack has had leadership positions in dozens of industry associations, alumni organizations, and charitable endeavors, including The Police Benevolent Association, St. Benedict's Catholic Church, and St. Mary's Hospital. We met up at Stella's on Lafayette Street.

I graduated from the University of Richmond in 1961, and received my MBA there in 1964. I went to work for George Wayne Anderson at Anderson & Strudwick, and soon after was offered a position on the trading desk with Dick Heward. Dick had been in the business in Philadelphia for years before coming to Richmond. In 1967, Dick and I went to Abbott, Proctor & Payne, one of the largest firms in Richmond at the time, to start a trading department for them. That firm ran into some financial problems and was bought by Paine Webber in 1970. I then accepted an offer from Mr. Freddie Bocock at Scott & Stringfellow, which I joined in 1970.

My father didn't have a direct influence on me being hired by Scott & Stringfellow, although his reputation certainly helped me in Richmond. Freddie Bocock wanted to become a bigger presence in trading, with the ability to trade stocks like Thalhimers, Miller & Rhoads, and local bank stocks, so he hired me to run a trading operation. The firm didn't make markets when I joined, and the trader was an older man who had been around a while. In the mid-1980s I brought over Dan Franks, who later became head of trading, and Jim White, from Wheat.

Scott & Stringfellow also expanded its investment banking capabilities, which meant we had to become more active trading stocks. When our bankers made a presentation to a company to help them raise money by selling stock, the bankers had to be able to tell the client that we would make a market in their stock. You couldn't compete for stock offerings if you couldn't trade the stock in the aftermarket.

The firm elected four new partners in 1972, and I was one of them. The others were Darrell Meade in operations, Bill Harsh in research, and Bernard Clary in the back office. We remained a partnership until 1974, after the death of Mr. Scott, when we incorporated.

We had six branch offices in 1974, with about seventy employees. David Plageman was hired around that time to oversee the branch system. Later, Bill Schubmehl, a good friend of mine, took over the branch management position. We made a few acquisitions and continued to grow.

We went public in late 1986 and used the capital to continue to grow, acquiring Independent Securities in Greensboro, Investment Corporation of Virginia in Norfolk, and Horner, Barksdale in Lynchburg. The added capital enabled us to underwrite offerings and make markets in securities. I had observed over the years that lack of capital could lead to big problems for firms that kept securities in inventory for trading purposes.

BB&T bought Craigie Inc., a Richmond bond dealer, in 1997, a year or so before they bought us. Craigie was the biggest municipal bond underwriter in Richmond, and also traded government securities. Craigie's headquarters were across the street from us. They moved into our building after our deal closed, and Scott & Stringfellow management ran the combined firms.

After the acquisition by BB&T, we cut back exposure in equities and bonds, across the board. BB&T is a good bank and the people are very good people, but they didn't like being exposed to the market risk.

Relationships were always an important part of the business. We had strong relationships with several firms in New York, such as Clark, Dodge, our correspondent. I've come to know a lot of people in the business through trade groups and industry organizations, which was rewarding personally, and for the firm.

You've known many accomplished veterans of Main Street finance outside of Scott & Stringfellow. Would you name a few?

I would say that one of them was Henry Valentine. Another was B. B. Munford. They worked side by side at Davenport.

Carlyle Tiller, who attended the University of Richmond, was chairman and chief executive officer at Wheat for many years. His brother, Bill, a self-educated man, was chief financial officer at Bank of Virginia. Their father died at an early age, and their mother did a pretty good job in raising them under difficult circumstances.

The Mutual Building was an icon on Main Street. Do you recall any anecdotes about the location that people may not remember today?

There's a story I've heard that, before my time, every morning and afternoon operations people would enter the vault, take securities out, and put them on a flat-bed cart. They'd lock the cart down and roll it down the hall to the bank and pull it right into their vault. A partner would walk behind them with a .38 long barrel—unloaded—for security. No one messed with them.   ■

LOUIS O. BOWMAN, JR.

Louis is a retired institutional salesman, most recently with Morgan Stanley. He connected top-ranked analysts at Dean Witter and Morgan Stanley with Virginia-based institutional investors who ordinarily did not have direct access to that quality of research. The analysts appreciated his professionalism, and the accounts respected his knowledge and contacts. I ran into Louis at Jim White's service in August 2017. Not too long after that, we sat down in the West End home where he lives with his wife Eve. "I've been retired for sixteen years. I still attend the Morgan Stanley shareholders' meeting every May. I decided a long time ago that some of my old colleagues should meet in New York in May and November, so I got all these people together, and most of us have never missed having a nice lunch together."

I started in the business in 1957, at Anderson & Strudwick, but was with them for only three months. Anderson & Strudwick had a great correspondent relationship, Carl M. Loeb Rhoades in New York, and I went up and interviewed with them. I worked there for three years. I was single and lived in New York City . . . a great experience. It gave me a lot of insight into how the stock market works.

I came back to Richmond between 1960 and '61 and worked for Anderson & Strudwick again. By then I had become registered with the New York Stock Exchange, and I had lots of contacts in New York through Loeb, Rhoades. All the contacts I made in New York helped me, and it helped the firm.

In the mid-1970s, I went to work for Dean Witter, which later became Morgan Stanley. All told, I was in the business a total of about forty-five years, with Loeb, Rhoades, Anderson & Strudwick, and Dean Witter, which became Morgan Stanley.

I was in institutional sales at Dean Witter. There were twenty-one institutional salesmen in New York, Wilmington, Richmond, Chicago, San Francisco, and Dallas. I still get together in New York with the sales and research people that we used to work with. Do you remember John Mendelson, Dean Witter's technical analyst? He comes for lunch when he's in town. He's retired, with homes in New York; Vero Beach, Florida; and New Hampshire, where the skiing is good.

I had a tremendous advantage with accounts because I often traveled with either a strategist, an economist, or an analyst. We visited various money managers and institutional investors. We would sit around a conference table, and the analyst talked about his industry. I wanted everybody to get to know my firm's analysts. We'd receive commission business in return.

Every year I would go to the Emporia Pork Festival. At that time, they'd sell fifteen thousand tickets in October for an event that took place the following June. It was really neat to be able to go to that. I would buy tickets, rent a small bus, and take many people who managed money in Richmond on the bus to the Emporia Pork Festival. A couple of my friends that I still talk to and meet for lunch in New York came down for it.

Who were some of your accounts?

I covered the Virginia Supplemental Retirement System. At that time it was about thirty-five billion dollars. It's now about eighty billion dollars, give or take.

One account in Norfolk was Virginia National Bank. There were other investment counseling firms in Norfolk and Lynchburg, and Roanoke has some fairly decent-sized investment counselors.

Now we have a lot of investment counseling firms here in Richmond, many established in the last four or five years. But one that was in Richmond when I was working was Lowe, Brockenbrough. Austin Brockenbrough and Jim Lowe started with just a handful of people in the Mutual Building. But they now manage a lot of money. Maybe two or three billion dollars, the last I heard.

Jack Maxwell, at Wheat, First Securities, was at one time the best tobacco analyst in the industry. *Institutional Investor* magazine ranked him highly. After a career in New York City, he came down here to live in Richmond. I think he lived at The Tuckahoe.

One of the things I did was to invite prominent financial analysts to speak at seminars in Richmond. One time the subject was coal. All the top coal analysts on the Street and in Richmond attended. We had probably 110 people from all over the world at that seminar.

I invited Charles Brown, the president of AT&T and a University of Virginia graduate, to speak at a meeting of the Richmond Society of Financial Analysts. AT&T was the largest company in the world at that time. In my introduction, I mentioned the fact that Mr. Brown was on the UVA baseball team. When he got up to speak, he said, "Louis, I'd like to tell everybody how good I was playing baseball, but I look out in the audience and I see Billy Hill, who was a great athlete at Virginia. I don't think Billy Hill would let me get away with that." Billy was the nicest guy. He worked for Wheat.

A year later I arranged for Cliff Garvin, the president and chairman of Exxon, the old Standard Oil of New Jersey, to present at one of our meetings. At that time, Exxon had grown to be the largest corporation in the world.

I invited Bill Johnston, the president of the New York Stock Exchange, to speak before the Richmond Society of Financial Analysts on September 11, 2001. I had known Bill for years, and knew that, as a graduate of Washington and Lee, he'd welcome the opportunity to visit with us in Richmond. Of course, Bill never did make it that day. He was in his limo on the way to LaGuardia to fly down here that morning when the first plane hit the tower. When the second plane hit, the limo turned around, and Bill made his way back to the Exchange.

I had known Bill for years, since my first visit to the floor of the Exchange when I was introduced to him. At the time, he was a specialist for LaBranche, a large market maker and specialist firm. He was responsible for trading several Virginia-based stocks, including Bank of Virginia, Best Products, Circuit City, and others. I would look Bill up every time I visited the floor after that, and we became friends. We rescheduled his Richmond presentation for later in the year, and it was quite successful.

By the way, I've always thought the floor of the New York Stock Exchange was a marvelous place, a miracle—the biggest marketplace in existence, where stocks from all over the world were bought and sold. I was thrilled every time I set foot there.

Stock market declines led to opportunities for future investing gains. New people with new ideas would come into the business. Some very smart people created a new product, the hedge fund, which changed the business. One of the first hedge funds was run by a man formerly with Loeb, Rhoades by the name of Michael Steinhardt. He's one of the most outstanding people in the investment business. He's still living; I saw him a year and a half ago at a reunion of ex-Loeb, Rhoades people.

You know lots of people in the business. Who are a few names from Richmond?

Stuart Seaton was the finest and most outstanding person I've ever known, always playing fair and by the book, and doing what was in the best interests of his clients. He was an airborne officer in the U.S. Army and retired as a full colonel. He came to Anderson & Strudwick after a twenty-one-year career in the army, the last two years as the senior artillery instructor at West Point. He was in the investment business for thirty-eight years, at Anderson & Strudwick and Dean Witter, and I worked with him for all of those years. You couldn't ask for a better person to work with.

There's a good story about Stuart's fiftieth birthday. To celebrate in style, I managed to borrow a wheelbarrow from the construction people working on what is now the SunTrust building next door. I put an Army blanket in it, wheeled it up to his desk, and told him to get in because we were going to the Bull & Bear Club for a few drinks. He wouldn't get in at first, but we talked him into it. We went down to the street, crossed Ninth Street, went to the service entrance at the Fidelity Building, and rode the elevator up to the club and bar. We encountered a few bumps along the way, but didn't want him to walk!

I knew Buford Scott. I also knew his father. And Mr. Edward Anderson and Edmund Strudwick, who had been with Scott & Stringfellow before they left to start up a new firm, Anderson & Strudwick. Oh, Jack Muldowney's father was with Scott & Stringfellow for a lifetime. Marvelous individual.

Homer Marshall was a real character. He was very knowledgeable about the bond business, and he had a lot of accounts who relied on him. I enjoyed working with him.

Charlie Mills was another guy who was a real character. Before he went into the investment business, he used to play cards and gamble. He learned a certain system. When he went into the investment business, he figured out another system. Charlie would look at financial statements from a certain company, and figure out what their *productive assets* were. He would sell this approach to individuals and institutions.

Charlie and I went to New York one time to meet with a huge account. We stayed at the Waldorf Astoria. Nothing was too good for Charlie Mills.

At any rate, the investment manager we saw liked the productive asset story. We kept in touch with this guy, and Charlie called him up one day and asked him to do some business. So the investment manager walked into his trading room and told his traders that he wanted to reward these two fellows in Richmond, so give them an order that would choke a horse. That afternoon, fortunately, the traders directed the order to Loeb, Rhoades. The order was 193,000 shares of a utility, the largest order I had ever had.

I was so excited about the order, I called one of the leading guys at Loeb, Rhoades who dealt with correspondents, and told him we had just traded 193,000 shares of such-and-such utility, and to please make sure the floor gives Anderson & Strudwick the credit. He asked if the trade was a buy or sell. I answered, "Jerry, I'm so excited about it, I don't remember whether it was a buy or a sell." He made one phone call down to the floor and came back and told me. I believe it was a sell.

DAVID S. ELLINGTON

Dave is a Financial Advisor with SA Stone Wealth Management. He's a big Virginia Tech fan, and sports fan in general. In fact, he was the varsity high school basketball coach for Lee-Davis High School for a year and assistant coach for many more. He's steady, honest, and has good judgment, which is why he's lasted so long in the business.

When I got out of college, my first job was working for the Richmond Times-Dispatch as a district manager. I was working the graveyard shift, and I didn't like that. A friend of my father's, Rod Brown, with Scott & Stringfellow at the time, said I should talk to them about getting into the financial services business. So I interviewed at Scott & Stringfellow, and Dean Witter, and I think one other firm, and ended up at Dean Witter. That was 1982.

I spent a month in Dean Witter's training class, about ninety people, in the World Trade Center in New York. After you got your license, they gave you a phone and a desk, and you went at it. You made lists of people to call every day. Being from Richmond, I knew what streets were well-to-do. We also got leads from Sears after they acquired Dean Witter. They weren't very good leads, but we got bonuses for opening accounts, even money market accounts.

You prospected with something conservative. Some of those tax-free bonds were yielding 10 percent. That was an unbelievable yield back then. Firms were beginning to come out with U.S. Government Ginnie Mae funds and other funds. These proprietary products were brand new to all of us. There was obviously price risk in them, but we were just selling the yield. And people were looking for yield.

It was a learning experience. You learn about risk. When you own an individual bond and hold it to maturity you should get your money back. With these funds, you couldn't guarantee that, really.

I remember buying some local small banks at Dean Witter. Investors Saving and Loan was one. It had been rumored, and had been in the newspapers, that Investors was an acquisition candidate. One of the brokers in the bullpen stood up and yelled "Investors Savings and Loan is having a board meeting right now. We need to buy the stock." We were calling people up and saying we think this company is going to be acquired, and you should buy it. We did right much business that day.

Dean Witter's compliance department got involved. In the end, we had to give back all our commissions. They said we were maybe trading on insider information. But we didn't have any inside information. This news was all over the city. Turns out, Investors wasn't bought out. Later, the Resolution Trust Corp. came in out of the blue one day and closed the doors.

Clyde Pitchford, what a story. I was a new broker, and my perception was that he was independently wealthy. He would have his Rolls-Royce come pick him up out in front of the office. It was strange. Back then, he was creating false customer statements. That wasn't an easy thing to do with the technology available back then, but he spent a lot of time to make them look legitimate. And he was sending the real ones to his own P.O. Box. I always thought if he had worked as hard on doing business right, he probably could have been successful. But his ego was bigger than his ethics.

I left Dean Witter in 1987 and went to Anderson & Strudwick to work with Charlie Mills. It worked out well. Back then, Charlie was a million-dollar producer, and that was huge. He gave us confidence to go in and buy when stocks crashed. I don't know whether I would have had that confidence at Dean Witter. You just didn't have that hands-on type of person involved. He might have saved my career.

What did you learn from Charlie?

I learned how to value—as best you can—companies, based on their assets. Charlie had a productive asset model that stripped out a lot of things that don't really produce earnings. He was more interested in hard assets. He worked extremely hard, and he was very bright. Charlie built concentrated positions in stocks and took a lot of risk at times. Sometimes they worked, and sometimes they didn't. But he had a lot of winners, though.

World Acceptance ended up being a huge winner for him, and us. In fact, I have accounts that still own World Acceptance. Their profits are so great we can't sell it. Pioneer Federal is another. They were acquired by Capital One. I have a client that bought Pioneer Federal Savings and

Loan, and now it's Capital One, and he still owns it and likes to look at it on his statement.

I had one of my biggest days in the business with another great story from Charlie: Freddie Mac preferred stock. At the time, only savings and loans could buy it.

That was probably '89 or '90. All savings and loans were struggling with bad loans at the time. Charlie convinced a lot of the savings and loans in town to buy as much Freddie Mac as they were allowed. At the time, S&Ls were limited as to how much they were allowed to buy. Regulators were going to make the stock available to the public, so ultimately everybody could buy it.

Charlie knew that, and made fifty million dollars for Pioneer Savings and Loan, which saved it. We invited every savings and loan in the area to a conference, where Charlie was going to talk to them about buying Freddie Mac. Only one or two people showed up. I met with Investors Savings and Loan, and they bought some stock. We made them twenty-five million dollars, but that didn't save them. If they had bought the maximum allowed, they would still be in business today. That was an unbelievable home run. When he could, Warren Buffett bought it, and it just skyrocketed.

We worked with a Dominion Resources investment officer, and he bought large amounts of stock. I think I had a fifteen-thousand-dollar commission day, which back then was absolutely huge. We made people a lot of money.

What was working at Anderson & Strudwick like?

It was much more entrepreneurial than the wire houses, and the ideas were more unique in nature. It was a great, great group of people. It's just the difference between being at a large institution and a small firm. Anderson & Strudwick was very small. It was very well known in Richmond. It was a good place to grow your business.

I never had more fun than working at Anderson & Strudwick. Ray Wood and Mike Via and all of us sitting around the trading desk . . . we had a good time.

After hours? O'Malley's was the classic. It's where I met my wife. Then there was Bus Stop and Sam Miller's. Monday night was tequila night at The Tobacco Company with Charlie. Back in the '80s, the community was a lot smaller, and we were all in the same area. If you recall, Bank of Virginia used to have Christmas parties for brokers and bankers at Eighth and Main.

Employees bought the firm from George Anderson after the Crash. Then, Anderson & Strudwick was acquired by Sterne Agee, a firm out of Birmingham, Alabama, around 2011. Sterne Agee was then bought by Stifel. A&S went through a lot of changes over the years, that's for sure.

I remained with Sterne Agee for a few years. Then a group of us decided to go independent. Sterne Agee had an independent side.

What does that mean, "go independent"?

There are two sides to the business. One is the private client group. With the private client group, the firm bears all business costs. They pay for your real estate, your phones. You get research. But you keep less of the revenue that you generate. On the independent side, we provide everything ourselves except compliance and clearing, and anything else we decide we want from the firm on an à la carte basis. If we want its research, we can get it. If we don't, we don't. And we keep a lot more of the revenue we generate.

The business has evolved, with indexing and exchange-traded funds that allow you to buy any sector you want. We use a lot of BlackRock and Vanguard. With my partner, Brad Brown, we do more planning—analyzing client assets and running stress tests.

For example, what if a two-year bear market starts the day you retire and walk out the door? How will your situation look like ten years down the road? Will you run out of money? We try to anticipate and plan for these scenarios. We don't chase returns. We're investing for twenty-five or thirty years, not the next two or three years.

And we work on fees, not commission. That's probably the biggest change. We charge a percentage of the assets that we manage. I think that's a much better way to do it, when you think about it. I believe the clients like it that way too. They know we're going to stay on top of their accounts. We're getting paid for how we do, not how many things we do.

Today, you have to have more assets under management to make a living, which fortunately over time, my partner and I have been able to achieve.

Tommy was born in Petersburg and raised in Dinwiddie County, Virginia, where his family has lived for generations. His knowledge of the Civil War and state and local history is encyclopedic. He's a big New York Yankee fan, because their Triple-A farm club, the Virginians, called Richmond home in the 1960s. We met at King's Barbecue in Petersburg, Virginia, for this interview.

I'm from southern Dinwiddie County and worked on our neighbors' and our farms until my senior year in high school. After attending the University of Richmond for two years, I worked for the governor of Virginia on his personal staff. After Governor Dalton's term was over, and while taking additional college courses part time in the early 1980s, I was looking for a full-time job. I saw an ad in the *Richmond Times-Dispatch* that piqued my interest. The ad called for twelve stockbroker trainees in the Richmond office of Dean Witter Reynolds to initiate a very unique project.

Dean Witter had just been bought by Sears to be the stock brokerage piece of their financial services strategy. Sears already owned a bank, a real estate broker, and an insurance company. Sears' plan was to put Dean Witter offices inside their stores nationwide, including the stores at Regency Square and Cloverleaf Mall in Richmond. Both were thriving and dynamic malls and stores at the time, though not so much today. Sears planned on placing six brokers in each store.

Our in-store Dean Witter recessed offices were basic. Each had a Quotron (stock quote machine), a desk, and a second room used for larger meetings, all of which were located right next to the Allstate insurance desk. The theory was that customers would buy their insurance at Allstate and then slip over to investigate investments. We'd each work one day a week at our assigned store, while working the other days at the regular DWR downtown branch office. I worked out of the Cloverleaf Mall store. Sometimes we would switch stores or days with other trainees or with longer-serving brokers from the DWR branch office.

The public response was overwhelming at first. People that normally wouldn't visit a downtown brokerage office because they might have felt a little intimidated were, as envisioned, more comfortable talking to a broker in a Sears store. It was a truly wonderful people-watching experience. You eventually saw just about everybody you knew come through those two Sears stores as the program aged.

Did you open many accounts?

The concept worked brilliantly for opening new accounts at first, because it exposed a whole class of people to investing, which was the whole point of Sears and Dean Witter breaking this new ground. Shoppers would stop and pick up a brochure. You could hear them talk to each other: "Oh, an IRA, I've heard of those." They wouldn't approach you at first, though. They'd put the brochure in their pocket or pocketbook and walk away.

Were there any flaws in the idea?

Two or three things happened that ultimately hurt the program, in my opinion. First, eventually you ran out of new potential customers walking into the store. There were only so many people coming in to buy a Craftsman screwdriver! So you ran out of new customers. And of course some people would come by and ask you where certain merchandise in the store was located. Lastly, other DWR brokers' clients would come in to check on their investments made through other DWR brokers. The other brokers' customers had all the time in the world to talk, because most were retired. Unfortunately, you had to spend time with them because you were representing the company, but ultimately it really cut into your own time to make an income for yourself.

It got a little frustrating after a while because the Allstate agents were cleaning up, as their current customers were renewing policies time after time. But, just maybe, over the long haul people were more inclined to buy insurance than stocks at Sears.

The initial public offering (IPO) market was on fire back then. Any personal recollections?

Dean Witter co-managed an IPO of a company called Worlds of Wonder. Their hot-selling product was Teddy Ruxpin, the talking teddy bear. We learned a day or two before the stock came to market that a few of the newer brokers were going to be able to get some shares at the IPO price, and in addition, all were encouraged to buy at the opening, even if they did not get IPO shares. Teddy Ruxpin had been a big-selling toy, and the numbers looked good. Our analyst liked it. It was a story that was easy to sell because everybody was familiar with Teddy Ruxpin. DWR really wanted their brokers to support the company-managed IPO.

New brokers did get some shares at the IPO price, and as encouraged, most bought more on the opening when it first started trading. As usual, the stock traded sharply higher during the first day, but with this deal no one knew what prices customers had paid for the shares, especially those shares bought at the opening. Due to trading volume, we did not receive purchase confirmations back until well after the market closed. It was a huge mess.

It turned out that the price many clients paid for the shares at the opening was a higher price than it ever traded at on the first day. The company's official position on the matter was that the customers were liable for whatever purchase price the confirmation dictated, even though the stock never traded at that price. I lost several clients and friends because of that fiasco. I never tried to buy an IPO at DWR after that.

Getting back to Sears, you mentioned you had some great walk-in accounts. Would you describe one?

Let me tell you about my favorite Sears client. He looked like he was straight off the farm, a huge man, probably six foot three or six foot four. He was in his mid-eighties, highly intelligent, barely spoke English, and was deaf as a post. He was an immigrant from Russia. He left his homeland right before the Russian Revolution in 1917. When I first met him at Sears, he was wearing bib overalls covered in grease.

As our relationship grew, he told me in his broken English about his memories of Russia as a child. In one story, the first and only word was "Tigers." I had no idea what he meant, and was confused. He then explained, "Ball go into woods, boy goes after ball, boy not come back. Tigers." Wow.

I really respected him, and I'll tell you why. He looked like he was from the farm (he actually owned a junkyard), but he had a net worth of probably five to ten million dollars. I once asked him how he came to America, and he said he took a boat to San Francisco, boarded a train, and went as far as the train went. He got off in Hopewell and settled in Richmond.

He literally arrived with nothing but the clothes on his back and a remembrance of tigers. Through sheer hard work, he achieved the American dream.

That is why I ultimately finished my degree at the University of Richmond, in banking (*cum laude*). I have always wanted to help a person with that kind of drive achieve the financial knowledge and dexterity needed to survive in today's environment. My career as a financial advisor and the people I met during that long-ago time was an experience that I will never forget. I would not trade having done it for the world.　■

Charlie is chairman of Mills Value Advisors, Inc. An influential stockbroker and analyst on Main Street, Charlie was perhaps best known for his early discovery of Freddie Mac preferred stock, a pick that rescued at least one local savings and loan. It was clear at our meeting that his confidence, energy, and love of the stock market has not diminished a bit.

I started in the business by continuing in my family's tradition as a gambler. My grandmother, who was very religious, had a dress shop in Lincoln, Nebraska. Wealthy women would get together and play bridge for very large sums of money, and that is how my grandmother made her living.

She was a bridge player; I was a poker player. I played poker all the time in college. And then in the military, I ran poker games on the USS *Saratoga*.

I got interested in stocks because I thought that was gambling as well. I recognized at that time no probability tables existed. People like Ben Graham would say, well, what you should do is buy stocks below their net working capital. That's great, but tell me what the return is if you would do that in every case for the last fifty years, and I can compute the odds. They never computed the probabilities on things they espoused.

I decided that I couldn't stay in the Navy because my wife would leave me if I went to sea again. I had to find a way to make a living. I decided I was going to figure out what the odds were in the securities business. I didn't know anything about securities. So I wrote down every idea. I read every book in the library in Norfolk. I came up to Richmond and read every book in the library here. The idea was not to get answers, but to get questions.

Then I put together this massive file on every major company that had existed since 1926 and all their financial reports. So when a particular author said that you should buy companies that had consistent earnings, I would know which company had consistent earnings. Then I would track the performance and see whether or not there were any probabilities. It took me several years and was intriguing and enjoyable.

Anyway, I got to leave the ship at some point and was on vacation with my wife. We went to this bar in Spain, where everyone spoke Spanish, which I don't speak. There was only one person there who spoke English. I was so excited to hear an American voice, I went over and talked to him.

We got drunk. Turned out that he was an accountant for a previous treasurer of the United States. He was complaining because he was losing so much money (it was 1970). I said, oh, you don't need to lose money. All you need to do is buy these, the ten most undervalued stocks on the New York Stock Exchange. I had that list. Now you just need to look at where the Dow Jones trades. Do not buy them until the index at the end of the month is higher than the previous six months. When that happens, buy these ten stocks. He laughed: "You couldn't do any worse than my brokers."

I thought I'd never see him again. It turned out he bought those ten stocks. They were up 70 percent by the time I got back to the States later that year. And he knew my name and the ship I was on and traced me back through his government contacts. I got a call from him, Mr. Collins, and he said, "I want more stocks."

I replied that I needed a place to get information. Brokers wouldn't let me go into brokerage houses and get all the current information and just hang around there.

He told me to not worry about that. If I told him where I'd like to go, he'd talk to the manager. So he called up the manager of Anderson & Strudwick, and gave him something like a million dollars' worth of trades and got him to hire me. That's how I got in the business.

Just a random meeting that I followed up on. A lot of success is very random, but you have to follow up. If there's a safety deposit key that you find when you're walking down the street, and it has a number, and it has the name of the bank, check it out and see what's in the safety deposit box. Don't ignore it.

I'd like to talk about a big stock in my career, Financial Corp. of America, a savings and loan in California and the largest in the country. In the early '80s, interest rates were going up. At that time, I had been recommending zero coupon bonds and Treasuries for conservative investors, and Financial Corporation of America common stock.

I was buying Financial Corporation and had built up a massive position for my clients at Scott & Stringfellow. Other brokers had large positions as well. Management was monitoring the situation closely, because at one point the stock was going down every day. If it went below five, it would be unmarginable. It was about six and a half at this point. Owning the stock was the right thing to do if you thought interest rates were going down.

What happened is interest rates did go down, and the stock went up 383 percent in the next year. Now of course we were on margin, so that was 700 percent for many of us. And it did better the following year, up another 386 percent. We made so much money for our clients. My personal commissions were approximately $1.5 million.

Any other interesting stories you were involved in?

Yes. How two billion dollars was made almost by accident.

Randy Whittemore, the president of Pioneer Federal, a local savings and loan, was an accountant and very, very diligent. I worked with him for years. He called me one day and said, well, we have a little bit more investment income because our Freddie Mac preferred stock increased its dividend.

I didn't want to insult Randy because, after all, he has a master's in accounting. But preferreds don't increase their dividends, as all stockbrokers know. They have a stated dividend. I knew he'd made a mistake. But I asked him to send me anything he had on that. So he sent me a report. What he had was called a *participating preferred* stock, which was popular in the Depression. If any dividend paid by the common stock was larger than the preferred, the preferred dividend would increase.

When I analyzed the company, it was the most undervalued stock, in my opinion, that had ever existed. Ever at any time in history.

At the time, only savings and loans or industrial banks could buy it. You couldn't buy it if you were a commercial bank, and you couldn't buy it if you were an individual investor or a corporation.

Savings and loans were in the process of going broke. Every single one of them was losing money during the savings and loan crisis. So the only accounts that could buy this stock were desperate, going broke, and they were selling their Freddie Mac stock to raise cash, depressing the price.

The stock was trading at three times earnings and paying an 8 percent dividend. It didn't have to pay to attract deposits because it had a charter with the government. Its profit margins were higher than any savings and loan or any bank. So I talked to my savings and loan clients in Virginia, and I was very effective in getting them to buy the stock. As a matter of fact, three savings and loans—Investors Savings and Loan, Virginia Beach Federal, and Pioneer—invested more than their total net worth.

I was perfectly happy owning these stocks and being responsible for putting the total net worth of the three largest savings and loans in central Virginia and Norfolk at risk, until I read in the paper that Congress, in its infinite wisdom, had allocated fifty million dollars to prosecute people who gave bad advice to savings and loans or banks that failed. Well, the thought occurred to me that I could go to jail if the stock went down.

I had been doing analytical work on deeply undervalued stocks for GEICO since 1979, and we made some money, but not a dramatic amount. But I begged Lou Simpson[23] to have Warren Buffett analyze Freddie Mac preferred. I wrote a little cover letter requesting him to ask Warren to look at the investment. It's sixty dollars. I believe it cannot be worth less than two hundred dollars. So I sent it out and Simpson told me that Buffett was pretty busy, and he'd get around to it. Didn't get a call the first week. The end of the second week, Lou called me and he said that Warren said it cannot be worth less than a thousand dollars a share. He started a massive buying program. They gave all the trades to us at Anderson & Strudwick.

What Warren Buffett did, while ownership was limited to 1 percent, was buy options for the right to buy Freddie Mac in the future, when you would be allowed to own more than 1 percent. The options were publicly traded. We did the trades. They'd just call us up and say, okay, we're buying X amount of options from X-and-so institution. They arranged the whole trade. All we did was collect the commissions.

In the end, Warren Buffett made two billion dollars on this idea, which is saying a lot. Freddie Mac was one of the six most profitable stocks he ever bought.[24] His return was 1,500 percent.

Great story. Any others?

There was a gentleman by the name of Dr. James Martin, a British citizen. He was doing some computer work for IBM in the United States.

It was kind of secret stuff. I found out about him from a stockbroker friend of mine. Dr. Martin had been buying my stocks for many years, all the way back to about 1977, '78, through my friend.

I started managing his money years later, and he gave me five million dollars to manage. My job was to buy interest-sensitive securities, because I was supposedly an expert in them, due to success with Freddie Mac and Financial Corporation and others.

I turned his five million dollars into three million dollars. I was summoned to Bermuda to see him. He looked at the numbers and said, "Charlie, do you need more money to work with?" I had just lost him two million dollars. Now, he had gone to Oxford on a full scholarship. His father was a factory worker and wouldn't support him at Oxford. But Dr. Martin was so grateful to Oxford for the assistance that he decided to pay them back. That's why he wanted to make money.

His commitment gave me the courage to take the necessary risk. The account went from three million dollars to over one hundred million dollars in eighteen months.

You really had to focus on his goal to make a big impact on Oxford. The money was not important to him unless it could fund the school. In fact, Dr. Martin ultimately became the largest donor to Oxford in its nine-hundred-year history. He ended up founding the James Martin School in Oxford and the James Martin Center for Nonproliferation Studies. He achieved all his goals.

It's November 2017. What's the most undervalued stock today?

Our largest position is PBR, Petrobras of Brazil. The stock's around $10\frac{1}{2}$. Its all-time high is 70.

IV

THE CLIENT

SAM E. SMITH, JR.

An expert shag dancer, beach music aficionado, and lifelong Clemson Tiger, Sam lives in North Myrtle Beach, South Carolina. He was a client of Clyde Pitchford, the Dean Witter and E. F. Hutton broker whose lavish lifestyle—a chauffeur-driven Rolls Royce, fox hunts, bespoke suits—was funded with clients' money, including Sam's. A riveting three-month search, with the FBI assisting, in 1986 led to Clyde's surrender in New York City, and national attention from People magazine, The Wall Street Journal, *and* The Washington Post.

My father passed away in '76, and he left us three boys a farm. We sold it and ended up getting seventeen thousand dollars each. I was living in Richmond working as a safety engineer for an insurance company at that time, and I didn't know what to do with that money.

One day I had to survey a business in downtown Richmond, and I saw a stock broker office, Dean Witter. I thought I'll just go in here and get some advice on what to do with this money. The receptionist at the front of the office recommended that I talk with a Clyde Pitchford. He opened an account for me and suggested a couple of stocks. I said, well, I'm trusting you. Let's see what happens.

Time went on, and I would call him or sometimes drop by the brokerage house. I considered him a friend. He would take me to see some horses he owned. He was also thinking about opening a restaurant in the Fan, called Humphrey's. I wanted to invest in it, but he kind of guided me away from that.

For our honeymoon, Clyde mailed me a key to a house he owned at Wintergreen and let my wife and I stay there for a week. I always wondered, why would he be so nice to me?

I called to speak with Clyde in 1986, at E. F. Hutton, his new employer, and was told that he didn't work there anymore, that they had a problem. I asked, a problem with what? I was told customer money was missing from some of Clyde's accounts, including mine. I wrote a letter insisting that they return my twenty-two thousand dollars, which the account was worth at that time, or I was going to take legal action. They didn't respond to that, and I wasn't happy. I felt I was being ignored.

By this time I had moved back to South Carolina. I was extremely worried about my money and didn't like the way things were being handled. I flew to Richmond, walked into E. F. Hutton, sat down in the branch manager's office, and got them to cut me a certified check for twenty-two thousand dollars. I wasn't going to walk out without it. It's really a shame, what happened to Clyde.

V

THE STRATEGISTS

W. ALLAN KEYES

Allan retired as chief investment strategist at The Trust Company of Virginia after serving for fifteen years as chief investment officer. A Virginia Tech Hokie, he and his wife Sue now live in Durham, North Carolina. We met many years ago through his college roommate and our mutual friend, Jim White. Allan serves on the board of directors of the Richmond Police Benevolent Association, and a visit to Richmond to attend one of their board meetings gave me an opportunity to sit down with him.

My career has involved managing both taxable accounts and tax-exempt accounts. I'm fortunate to have met many outstanding people who shaped my career, those I worked with and those I worked for. People like Harvie Wilkinson, John Blackwell, Ross Walker, Erwin Will, and Stuart Sachs. The investment business gave me the opportunity to meet some exceptional people, whom I may never have met otherwise.

How did you get started in the business?

Around 1967, after college and the service, I came back to Richmond and got to know Ross Walker, the senior partner of Abbott, Proctor, and Paine, a regional broker-dealer. Mr. Walker was highly respected, and while there were those around him then who called him Ross, I was not one of them. He was always Mr. Walker to me.

One day Mr. Walker came to me and wanted to know if I would help him as an assistant. There may have been some grumbling about the fact that I was relatively new to the firm and was sitting right outside the senior partner's office, but that quickly went away. I learned an awful lot about portfolio management with him. Mr. Walker, while being a senior partner in that regional house, did a lot of commission business, but he really taught me about portfolio management along the way.

Within the first year we lost a number of employees and clients in our Asheville, North Carolina, office. Mr. Walker asked me if I would consider moving to Asheville to help stabilize the office. So I moved to Asheville and stayed there three or four years. By the way, it's a beautiful part of the world and was a great place to live.

At some point I realized I wasn't particularly fond of the fact that the salesmen were too often worried about what their commission was on a trade rather than whether or not Mrs. Jones should own X, Y, or Z. So I began thinking about moving to the so-called *buy side*, switching from managing taxable money for individuals to managing institutional assets, foundation endowments, and employee benefit plans.

I had a couple of interviews, one at First & Merchants and another with Capitoline Investment Services, the investment management subsidiary of United Virginia Bankshares. I decided to join Capitoline, working for Erwin Will, who put together quite a successful team of portfolio managers and analysts. Later, First & Merchants offered me a position managing tax-exempt money, and I accepted the offer and worked there for a number of years. That position was a pivotal turn that led me to eventually join The Trust Company of Virginia.

When I started at First & Merchants, John Blackwell headed the trust department. He was six foot five and was affectionately referred to as "Tall Man." I'd only been there a few days when he came into my office on the twelfth floor. My office had massive doors, twelve-foot doors, to be exact. He came in and asked if he could sit down for a second, and he did.

Mr. Blackwell said that while he knew I was there to manage institutional money, he wanted me to consider managing the assets for at least one family that's very prominent here in Richmond, and I agreed.

When he got up to leave, he grabbed the door handle and pulled it when he needed to push. So help me, it turned into a two- or three-minute spectacle of Mr. Blackwell trying to get out of my office. He was bound and determined to pull that door almost off its hinges, which would have been impossible. He finally realized the error of his ways and pushed the door. He turned around and suggested that I'd get used to the pull-push of the doors around the place.

I thought to myself, well, Tall Man's been here ten years, and *he's* not used to it yet!

I then spent a brief period at Mentor Investment Group, a subsidiary of Wheat, First Securities, where I was given the opportunity to head

Date: April 1, 1998
DJII: 8,799.81

ANDERSON & STRUDWICK
INCORPORATED

RESEARCH

WRITTEN PURCHASE RECOMMENDATION RECORD
OF CHARLES A. MILLS, III

Investments Maturing/Held One Year	S&P 500 Average	$100 Invested	Recommended Average	$100 Invested
1980	+ 15%	$115.00	+ 53%	$ 153.00
1981	+ 2%	$117.30	+ 2%	$ 156.06
1982	- 12%	$103.22	+ 63%	$ 254.38
1983	+ 35%	$139.35	+141%	$ 613.05
1984	+ 2%	$142.14	- 24%	$ 465.92
1985	+ 15%	$163.46	+ 32%	$ 615.01
1986	+ 27%	$207.59	- 20%	$ 492.01
1987	+ 25%	$259.49	+178%	$ 1,367.79
1988	- 11%	$230.45	+ 2%	$ 1,395.14
1989	+ 22%	$281.76	+ 98%	$ 2,762.38
1990	+ 1%	$284.58	+ 9%	$ 3,011.00
1991	+ 14%	$324.42	+ 59%	$ 4,787.49
1992	+ 18%	$382.81	+ 49%	$ 7,133.35
1993	+ 10%	$421.10	+ 42%	$10,129.36
1994	+ 1%	$425.31	+ 42%	$14,383.69
1995	+ 24%	$527.38	+ 37%	$19,705.65
1996	+ 20%	$632.85	+ 48%	$29,164.36
1997	+ 30%	$822.71	+ 36%	$39,663.53

1. The above is a constructed index outlining the return of stocks recommended by Charles A. Mills, III assuming that the stocks were held for one full year and were sold at month end. The S&P 500 average return is calculated over the same holding period of the purchase recommendation. We assume an equal weighted purchase of recommended securities and the S&P 500 Index.

2. This is a research recommendation track record, not an investment track record.

3. The S&P 500 is an unmanaged index. We publish this data to refute the commonly held academic position which states that all information of value concerning a stock is reflected in its current price. We believe that excess returns can and will be generated by a commitment to fundamental analysis.

4. The period covered was one of generally rising markets. There is no guarantee that past performance will equal future performance. Underperformance can occur at any time.

5. S&P 500 Index data courtesy Bloomberg Financial Markets..

Additional information is available upon request.

ANDERSON & STRUDWICK IS AN EMPLOYEE OWNED COMPANY
ACCOUNTS PROTECTED TO $25 MILLION*

Anderson & Strudwick

707 East Main Street

Richmond, Virginia

23218

804/643-2400
800/767-2424
Fax 804/343-3308

Richmond
Charlottesville
Fredericksburg
Norfolk
St. Augustine, FL

1948 - 1998
50
YEARS OF
EXCELLENCE

NYSE
Member New York
Stock Exchange

Charlie Mills' remarkable stock recommendation track record.

Jerry Epperson's furniture research: the best in the industry.

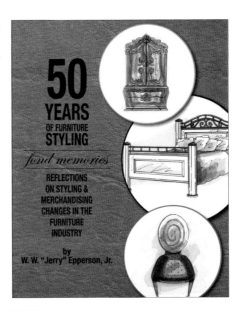

Did Merrill Lynch begin in Richmond? Sign outside Merrill's Washington, D.C., office, early 1980s, said it did.

W. T. O'Malley's, a
Main Street favorite,
where Chip Mann, in
between political gigs,
waited on politicos
and financiers.

Former State-Planters Bank Building, Ninth and Main Streets.
Built in 1926, now used by the Commonwealth of Virginia.

Broker is object of search

By Rob Walker
Times-Dispatch staff writer

New York City police, friends, relatives and co-workers are looking for Clyde B. Pitchford Jr.

An account executive with the Richmond office of E.F. Hutton & Co. Inc., Pitchford, 31, has not been seen

Richmond Times-Dispatch

February 23, 1986

Clyde Pitchford headlines captivated Richmond in 1986. Vendors capitalized on stockbroker Pitchford's disappearance.

The Richmond Stock Exchange's 1947 by-laws filled just a few pages. Many of the member names have been familiar to Main Street for generations.

OFFICIAL RICHMOND STOCK EXCHANGE
MEMBERSHIP

Members	*Representatives*
Abbott, Proctor & Paine	Caskie G. Burch
	Russell C. Williams
Branch & Co.	Edmund A. Rennolds, Jr.
Branch, Cabell & Co.	Cary Stewart Shield
	Mason New
	Roderick D. Moore
Davenport & Co.	Robert P. Martin
	Coleman Wortham, Jr.
	William Frazier
	Beverley B. Munford
Miller & Patterson	L. Gordon Miller
Mason-Hagan, Inc.	Homer L. Ferguson, Jr.
Scott & Stringfellow	Buford Scott
	Edward C. Anderson
	Thomas D. Neal
	Joseph Muldowney

President
L. GORDON MILLER, Miller & Patterson

Vice-President
HOMER L. FERGUSON, JR., Mason-Hagan, Inc.

Secretary-Treasurer
JOSEPH MULDOWNEY, Scott & Stringfellow

[16]

Sales avalanche sends
Dow to a record loss

From wire dispatches

NEW YORK — An avalanche of selling pounded stocks and dealt the Dow Jones industrial average its first loss of more than 100 points yesterday, but the bond market was left unscathed by the turbulence.

Already off sharply in the preceding two sessions, stock prices fell into a steep decline yesterday. The Dow Jones industrials plummeted a record 108.36 points to 2,946.73, a level not seen since May.

below 2,300 about two-thirds of the way through the session. It bounced briefly, then headed lower again. Minutes before the close, the Dow average was down nearly 130 points.

Trading volume on the New York Stock Exchange soared to a record 338.48 million shares, surpassing the previous high of 302.39 million set

from 299.13 million Thursday.

Two other market indexes also plunged. That of the American Stock Exchange dropped 12.25 to 323.55 while the National Association of Securities Dealers fell 16.18 to 406.33. Composite volume on the Amex rose to 21.82 million shares from 14.63 million Thursday.

The drop yesterday wiped out $145 billion in the value of stocks, according to the Wilshire Associates index, which accounts for about 5,000

Brokers comment, A-10

Richmond Times-Dispatch   *October 17, 1987*

'Buying panic' lifts Wall Street

Greenspan's comment spurs 380.53-point rise

BY BOB RAYNER
TIMES-DISPATCH STAFF WRITER

For weeks, they've been yelling "Fire!" on Wall Street, and investors have been racing for the door.

Yesterday, someone yelled "Fire sale!" and they came rushing back in, pushing the Dow Jones industrial average up 380.53 points, its biggest single-day points gain ever. The closely watched Nasdaq composite also turned in its best-ever one-day gain, up 94.34 points.

Richmond Times-Dispatch

September 9, 1998

Above: The DJIA lost more than 100 points for the first time on Friday, October 16, 1987. The following Monday the DJIA crashed, dropping 508 points, or 23%.

Left: On September 8, 1998, the DJIA gained 5%, or 380 points (a point record at the time), on favorable inflation comments from the Fed chairman. Another record was smashed that day, when Mark McGwire hit his 62nd home run.

Bullpen, Wheat, First
Securities, May 6, 1987.

Scott & Stringfellow's
iconic Dow Jones
Industrials electronic
sign graced the Mutual
Building from 1970
until the firm moved
to the Riverfront
Plaza in 2010.

Sears Will Purchase Dean Witter In Plan to Offer Financial Services

By ROBERT J. COLE

Sears, Roebuck & Company, the nation's biggest retail store chain, announced yesterday that it would buy Dean Witter Reynolds Inc., the fifth-largest brokerage house, for about $607 million in cash and stock.

The acquisition is a major step in the Chicago-based retailer's stated goal of becoming the "largest consumer-oriented financial service entity" in the

marks the third time this year that a major American corporation has undertaken to acquire a top brokerage house in the new competition among major corporations to provide comprehensive financial services.

For Sears, it was the third financial venture announced in the past month. Earlier this week, it reached agreement to buy Coldwell, Banker & Company, a

The New York Times

October 9, 1981

Sears announced the purchase of Dean Witter Reynolds in 1981 for $600 million.

Wall Street Deli,
Eighth and Franklin.

all of portfolio management. I enjoyed my stay, though short, at Mentor, but The Trust Company of Virginia, which started just a year earlier, made an overture to me. They offered me the chief investment officer position, and I took it, which is where I finished my career.

The reality is that the CIO of the firm has to guide the management of money, and in so doing, has to manage people and the investment process. Eventually, I had five or so people in the investment area. The personalities were A-types, bright and aggressive, and managing them was something I had to get used to.

For most of my career, I was fortunate to work with and for people of substance, talents, and skills in the financial services industry. This helped me discharge two of the most important tasks for a CIO: successfully managing people and, equally important, managing the investment process. Identifying, building, and executing an appropriate investment style and methodology might well be the most important job for a chief investment officer—never to be treated lightly. This is so because the outcome goes a long way to help identify and quantify levels of expected risk and returns in portfolios.

Each job carried more responsibility and visibility than the previous one.

I think that's accurate—the big move was going from the sell side to the buy side. While I was not particularly enamored with selling securities and was not necessarily a great sales person, I had a lot of friends on the sell side and respected what they do.

Selling securities is no easy task. I was always impressed with salesmen at full-service research houses who were able to talk knowledgably about all the industries covered by their analysts. By comparison, analysts themselves had to understand just the one or two industries or sectors they followed. It would be hard enough for you or me just to know what you needed to know about the one sector that you specialized in, much less every other sector followed by your firm.

The 1987 Crash? Although I was standing on the ledge, I was of the opinion that it was overblown. Market participants, especially those with a short-term horizon, make it easy to overstate these things. As long as our economic system is producing earnings growth and the system remained intact, we'll have recessions and so forth, but naysayers will be sorry that they're selling instead of buying. In all prior hiccups—that was certainly more than a hiccup, of course—the buyers seemed to fare better than the sellers.

Whose opinions did you particularly value?

The Trust Company of Virginia utilized maintenance research from larger firms, special equity research from smaller firms, and economic analysis. Economic analysis was most important to me as chief investment officer, to help form my views and forecasts. Ed Hyman at ISI, and Jason Trenert of Strategas, were exceptional people, and good with markets and economic policy.

I know that you and Jim White, who recently passed away, were famous friends.

We were. Much of Jimmy's trading career dealt with management of the firms where he worked and their understanding of the trading function. Sometimes he became frustrated. For example, there was a very high-profile individual at that time on Main Street, who would walk into the trading room in the morning, look at the quote machines, and ask the traders what certain stocks were going to do that day. Jimmy White would wonder, in amazement, how a serious person who knew anything about markets could ask that question.

As Jimmy reminded me, a trading function is simply balancing supply and demand and establishing a price. Insofar as walking into the trading room and asking about what X, Y, or Z is going to do that day, traders may answer we think it's weaker, or something like that, and then you'd shuffle off. But this guy really did believe that the traders knew what stocks were going to do every day. And Jimmy just couldn't get over that. It was just beyond his ability to understand that a management-level person would think you could know what stocks would do in advance.

Jimmy always wanted to know what buy-side and sell-side investors thought about stocks. What does the smart money like, and what don't they like? Jimmy and I used to laugh all the time about how crazy this business is. No matter what stock someone likes and thinks we should own, there is somebody who thinks it should be sold right now. That's what makes markets tick.

Is there a correct opinion about Coca-Cola on any given day? The answer is of course not. There are sell recommendations and there are buy recommendations. We used to tell our clients over and over there is no correct answer. It's only opinion. ▪

Jeff, chief investment strategist for Raymond James Financial, Inc., is a frequent commentator on CNBC and other television and print media. Jeff spent many years on Main Street in Richmond in various sales and research capacities. As director of research for Ferris, Baker Watts in Baltimore, Jeff recruited several Richmond-based capital markets professionals to FBW in the 1990s. I visited Jeff in his home in the Old Northeast neighborhood in St. Petersburg, Florida.

I started in New York City in 1971 on a trade desk for a hundred bucks a week. The market opened at 10:00 a.m. and closed at 3:30 p.m. The traders sent me out every morning at 9:30 a.m. for coffee and Danishes to bring back to the trade desk. For six months, I walked by my boss's office, and I always noticed a big red number "4" on the wall behind his desk above the credenza. Finally, I got up enough courage to ask, Mr. Mayer, what's the deal with the big red "4"?

And he got this big smile on his face and said, "Kid, that's the number of bear markets you're gonna see in your career. Don't ever forget it." And I never forgot it. So let's count: '73/'74; '80 to '82; 2000 to late 2002, early 2003; and late '07 to early '09. How did he know in 1971 I would see four bear markets? I got real lucky because the trade desk manager quit in Atlanta, and I was the only one in the organization with a Southern accent, so they sent me to Atlanta to run the trade desk.

Things were getting really nasty in late '72, early '73, and I went to work for E. F. Hutton in '73. Right when the market was dropping from 1,051 to 577, the closing low on, I believe, December 6, 1974. I wrote my first strategy report then. It basically said stocks are trading below all known values. Now is the time to start accumulating equities. Nobody wanted to buy because you could get 9 or 10 percent or something like that in a money market account.

My wife Cheryl and I quit our jobs in November 1975 and moved to Aspen. We didn't work. All we did was ski. And then I came to Richmond, Virginia, and went to work for Thomson McKinnon, a fine firm in its day before being blown up by a few people at the top. It was a fairly big firm back in the day. I worked for them from '76 to probably '85.

During that whole period, I wrote strategy reports for the firms I worked for. I think my last production year in the business was 1985, and

I did $727,000 worth of business, which was a big number back then. It would be like three million bucks today. So nobody really said anything to me when we would take off for extended vacations.

Wheat, First Securities took notice of me and brought me in as an institutional sales person and gave me Florida as a territory which, quite frankly, didn't have very many accounts in it. But I did institutional sales for them for a year. Then Tom Dorsey and Watson Wright created Dorsey Wright, which was the charting service using X's and O's, point and figure, three-point-reversal charts. And they went out on their own.

Art Huprich and I were the only people left at the firm who had what was known in the day as Bridge Data machines. Wheat asked me if I would take over the technical analysis department, which I did, even though I'd been trained by my dad as a fundamental analyst.

Right before the Crash of 1987, I got in some hot water because I had said weeks earlier in *Barron's* that I think we're going to get a waterfall decline.[25] I told people to either hedge their positions or sell some stocks and raise some cash. At Wheat, First Securities, you weren't supposed to use the dreaded four-letter-word *sell*. So their main strategist got upset with me and told me to toe the line, which I wouldn't. In any event, they pushed me out of Wheat, First Securities, which turned out to be one of the best moves of my career.

I went to work for Branch, Cabell as director of research. Some of the finest people I've ever worked with were at Branch, Cabell on Main Street in Richmond. Leighton Huske was a prince to me. Mason New was the CEO. It was a fine group of people, honorable people. You didn't need contracts. You looked them in the eye and shook their hand, and that was it. That's all you needed. It was like when I first got in the business in 1971. We didn't have employment contracts and all that stuff.

I then went to work as director of research at Ferris, Baker Watts in Baltimore, helping build capital markets with Todd Parchman. In 1995, Jim Holbrook from Sterne, Agee & Leach asked me to put together their capital markets operation. I did, and it was profitable in eighteen months, which was unheard of in that short period of time.

I've been very lucky. I started doing media on Ted Turner's channel 17 in '74 in Atlanta, and I've done media just about ever since. I was on *Wall Street Week* with Lewis Rukeyser. And I've done mainstream TV—

NBC, ABC. But for the past twenty years or thereabouts, I've been doing CNN, CNBC, Fox.

Do you enjoy appearing on CNBC the most?

CNBC has the widest viewership. It's allegedly worth one hundred thousand dollars in advertising for an appearance.

So Raymond James loves it.

I'm in the print media too, including *The Wall Street Journal*. Right over against that wall is a full interview with me in *Barron's,* talking about the secular bull market with years left to run.[26] I've made a lot of pretty good calls. I've made some bad calls. But one of the things my dad taught me—he said, "Son, if you think it's going up, be bullish. If you think it's going down, be bearish. But for gosh sakes, make a call."

I don't let investments go against me very far. I either sell a bad position or I will hedge if the fundamentals are still intact. My best stock? Probably Raymond James stock. Raymond James, after the public offering in 1983, has compounded at about 18 percent per year. Raymond James stock made a lot of people millionaires.

I'm real fortunate in that I talk to portfolio managers that have to put money to work. I was an analyst like you were. I've been a portfolio manager. I've been director of research at five firms, head of capital markets at three firms. So when somebody gives me an idea, I can spend thirty minutes on FactSet and decide if I want to buy the stock or not.

If I could have only one tool to make money with, it would be the telephone. Because if I want to know what's going on in semiconductors, I can pick up the phone and call the CEO of a semiconductor company. Or Tom O'Halloran, one of the best large-cap growth managers I know. He runs the Lord Abbett Growth Leaders Fund, which I own. I tend to invest in mutual funds where I know the portfolio manager. I can pick up the phone and call him. I don't tweet, I don't LinkedIn. I don't Facebook. But I own Facebook stock because Tom O'Holloran told me to buy it for my own account.

Mary Lisanti, I've known her for a long time. She's one of the best small-cap growth stock pickers I know. She was an institutional all-star at E. F. Hutton. Very smart.

Jeff, are there any Richmond-based publicly traded companies that you recall as good investments?

Yes. I wrote bottom-up fundamental research on individual companies before devoting all my time to strategy. I wrote on Markel, a great company. Tom Gayner still runs their investment portfolio and is the CEO. S&K Famous Brands. Circuit City, where Rick Sharp was CEO. Lawyers Title, the title insurance company. A couple of institutions paid me soft dollars, big orders, to go and sit in the first trials for the A. H. Robins Dalkon Shield and provide them with an opinion. I also wrote on Universal Leaf, the tobacco people. It was a nice company. Highly profitable. And Dibrell Brothers out of Danville.

Main Street was a pretty tight-knit group of people. Whitey Lipscomb at Craigie and Company was one of the bond kings back then. Coley Wortham at Davenport & Company was another standout. One of the brightest guys on Main Street was Mike Beall, a very good investor at Davenport. A really smart, good guy.

I don't think the business is as much fun as it was in the 1980s and 1990s. It was a real relationship business back then. When you deal with institutions now, it's not really a relationship business anymore. They're measuring you on execution, accuracy of earnings, estimates, and how you rate your stocks

I haven't worked in Richmond, Virginia, since 1992 or 1993. But I have very fond memories of the Anderson & Strudwicks and the Branch, Cabells, Craigie and Company. Even Wheat, First Securities. Very fond memories of those years in Richmond.

VI

THE ANALYST

WALLACE W. "JERRY" EPPERSON

Jerry is an award-winning managing director of furniture research at Mann, Armistead & Epperson, Ltd. He contracted polio in 1950 and gets around today almost exclusively by wheelchair and walker. He doesn't waste one second complaining about his situation. In fact, with his wit and optimism, you feel better yourself after talking to him. You'll also realize he's supremely self-confident, smart, and competitive. I wish I could include here some of his funnier R-rated stories about colleagues of days gone by. I also can't wait for him to finally finish the autobiography he started years ago, Limping Through Life in Crippling Detail.

I suffered my first year at UVA and quickly learned how my rural high school education, with a graduating class of fifty, was not competitive with other first-year men. I failed my first class ever, but I recovered in my second year, thanks to economics. I loved it. When I got an A, my father told me, "That's God telling you something. Go down that path." The same was true with accounting. It was difficult to believe others found accounting hard.

My two years in the McIntire School of Commerce taught me a lot, but when I neared graduation in the recession of 1970, job offers were not plentiful. No, I did not want to get into a bank training program or sell insurance. So, I went to the College of William & Mary to get an MBA. My experience in Charlottesville got me all As, with one B+ in Williamsburg. I should have gotten all As, but it's a long story.

I was fortunate to get an interview with Scott & Stringfellow, the well-known brokerage firm in Richmond. With my background in Victoria, Virginia, I had no experience with investments, but I enjoyed the investment and investment banking classes I had taken over the previous years. Some of the finest people I have ever met interviewed me. Buford Scott, Fred Bocock, and Bill Harsh took me out to lunch down in Shockoe Bottom. I remember them asking me if I wanted to go to the Commonwealth Club and be impressed or to have good food. We decided on good food. Henry Spalding, the partner in charge of research, soon called me to offer the job as an analyst working for Bill Harsh, and I accepted gladly.

At that time, furniture stocks were hot. The seventy-seven million post-war baby boomers were just getting out of school and starting households, and we had two years where housing starts exceeded two million units. My father, a conductor on the railroad that went from my hometown westward through several furniture towns, knew a lot of the furniture factories and how they were doing, which helped me. At that time, Wheat, First Securities had the leading furniture analyst, John McDowell, and I was told to learn all I could about the industry. Levitz was one of the hottest stocks at that time, with a 120-plus multiple, and it carried other public companies along, including Bassett, Lane, and others. Heilig Meyers, Flexsteel, La-Z-Boy, and others went public, and we assisted in some and took Pulaski public ourselves.

I was encouraged to visit and learn about all the public furniture manufacturers and retailers, about fifteen companies at the time. If I remember correctly, my manufacturer universe was American of Martinsville, Bassett, Berkline, Burris, Cochrane, Delwood, Ethan Allen, Flexsteel, Hickory, Henredon, Kroehler, Lane, La-Z-Boy, Pulaski, and Rowe; the retailers included Heilig Meyers, Haverty, and Levitz along with RB on the West Coast. These were people I was very comfortable with, often located in small towns. They quickly became friends. The stories I could tell about some of these folks!

My father's work on the railroad was especially helpful with Mr. Ed Lane, the founder of The Lane Company in Altavista, Virginia. Mr. Lane liked to ride in the caboose with my father, which was against the rules, but he was also a large customer of the N&W Railroad. He introduced me to some of his family and that helped me meet others, including some of the private companies. Only 30 percent of furniture manufacturers were public, and less than 15 percent of retailing firms were public, so it was important to know the private companies, too. All this helped me get very comfortable with the furniture industry. One of Mr. Lane's sons, B. B., was married to a Bassett daughter, allowing introductions there.

Meanwhile, Bill Harsh, the Director of Research, taught me how to be an analyst and had me do a lot of reading. I learned to hate *The Wall Street Transcript* because I had to read it and give Bill a synopsis of what was in it every week. Scott & Stringfellow had a couple of analysts, and I met more through the local Financial Analysts' Society. Bill encouraged me to earn my charter and become a Chartered Financial Analyst®. This intense three-year course, covering everything from analysis, accounting, government regulations, and ethics, to how to really interpret corporate annual reports and filings, gave me the deep background that helped me understand the investment business. Also helping was Scott & Stringfellow being a relatively small firm with about one hundred employees and six branch offices around Virginia. When different departmental heads were gone, I took their roles for the day, so I learned trading, compliance, capital markets, and other roles. You could not get a finer or broader education. Being a small firm, it was very much like family. I still remember going to partners' homes each Christmas, and a special treat was going to Royal Orchard, the Scott family castle brought over from Scotland to a huge site on the eastern side of Afton Mountain, just west of Charlottesville. One happy day was the first time I was quoted in *The Wall Street Journal*'s "Heard on the Street" column. It was a first for both me and the firm.

Compensation at Scott & Stringfellow changed when I was named an officer and allowed to buy some equity. I didn't have the money to buy hardly any, so my annual bonus was limited by my lack of equity. I did not see how I could buy more equity with such a limited bonus participation, so when I got a call from a friend at the Bank of Virginia, I listened. Wheat, First Securities was a much larger firm, with nearly a thousand employees and branches around both Virginia and North Carolina. There was an agreement between the two firms not to steal each other's employees. My friend at Bank of Virginia told me that Wheat had fired John McDowell, largely because of his bad experience with REITs, and they needed a furniture analyst. I made a call and learned that Mr. Jim Wheat knew of me because he was on The Lane Company board, and they made me an offer that gave me a participation in all the revenues I produced.

By now, I had been publishing research in the furniture industry for five years, including some large studies with a multiple regression analysis on the driving factors in furniture revenues, profits, and stock prices. I had been invited to speak at the largest furniture association's annual meeting where I did a horrible job, being so nervous. Thankfully, many felt sorry for me and later became good friends. I learned to become a good speaker and have now spoken to hundreds of conventions and meetings around the globe on the only thing I know: home furnishings. I had also started a monthly research service on what was going on with the public furniture companies and the furniture divisions of conglomerates like Singer, Congoleum, Mohasco, Scott Paper, Champion International, Burlington, Arkansas Best, Sperry & Hutchinson, Armstrong Cork, Household Finance, Wickes, Portland General Cement, and many others. It got a lot of interest, and I became a popular person to interview in the trade and financial press.

Maybe this would be a good spot to mention that I contracted polio in 1950 when I was two years old. It impacted me in many ways, with the most obvious being a paralyzed left leg. I could walk for years using braces, crutches, and canes, but it was something that made me different from others and easy to recognize. In 2006, after breaking my left leg three times in one year, I stopped walking and now only move about in wheelchairs and scooters. I miss walking, but I don't miss falling down often.

Moving to Wheat, First Securities on April 1, 1976, was a challenge. It was like leaving home and people you cared for. Wheat was huge in comparison, with branch offices in Hickory, Greensboro, Winston-Salem, Morganton, and Charlotte, North Carolina, as well as in Roanoke and Martinsville, Virginia, all of which are important furniture hubs.

Trust me, I did not know anyone at Wheat, and the research department had about a dozen analysts, not the few we had at Scott & Stringfellow. So I was anxious. Because they were out of room and were making plans to move soon into the new Eighth & Main Building, my first office was a glorified closet that I shared with the photocopier. At least I got to know a lot of the staff.

The first week there, Jack Kawa, Wheat's retail and coal analyst, invited Kathy and me to his home for dinner. That weekend, with Jack, his wife and his two daughters, a very cordial Jack explained that we could be friends away from work, but at the office we were competitors, and every bonus dollar you get is a dollar that I should have gotten. He explained we were competing for speaking time on the morning calls to the branches and to institutional sales, and to get the all-important commission dollars that determined much of the bonus pool. He also explained that the stocks he was following were relatively large market cap stocks that were actively traded, while most furniture stocks were very small in comparison. It was a truthful but scary conversation.

Topping all this, my stocks had fallen out of favor with Wall Street after the 1975 recession. As an example, in 1972 we announced an underwriting for Pulaski Furniture, which was trading at $18 a share. By the time of the offering it was over $30, and within eighteen months it hit $70. Its largest customer, Levitz, missed some of its estimates and Pulaski's stock fell sharply, reaching $3 a share in about a year. All of the other furniture stocks fell, although few as severely as Pulaski. Furniture stocks are cyclical and reliant upon the housing sector, so I had to wait until a recovery was evident to pound the table on my stocks. Let's face it, furniture stocks are either hot or dead.

I was watching our bank analyst, with all the locally held banks, and Lou Hannen, our utility analyst, with all the big power companies. The one thing I had going for me was that conglomerates were continuing to acquire furniture companies, hoping to benefit long term from all the baby boomers as they moved to larger homes and had children. If I received 100 percent of all the trades in my stocks, it would be small in comparison to the potential trades the other analysts had going for them.

Jim Wheat called me into his office one day in 1978 and said let's start a furniture services group to do mergers and acquisitions, financings, and valuations. He brought in Ed Crawford from North Carolina and a couple of others and said we're going to take Epperson's knowledge and exposure and leverage it to do deals. And it worked. In 1979, we were doing a deal a month. Were they huge deals? No, but they had cash fees of $150,000 to $350,000 or so.

Most of the time I earned between 10 and 15 percent of the banking fee from an acquisition or public offering. On a three-hundred-thousand-dollar fee, I might get thirty thousand dollars. There wasn't another person in our department who ever received a bonus for thirty thousand dollars. I've got a picture of Jack McElroy giving me the biggest bonus check that Wheat had ever written to a salaried employee, over fifty thousand dollars.

You would have thought I was robbing the bank. The other analysts starting raising hell that I'd found a way to make money that they couldn't. I was in an industry that was growing and consolidating. Some of these conglomerates that had bought furniture companies wanted out, and some of the companies that weren't in the furniture industry wanted in. The companies that were in the industry wanted to grow bigger. We just capitalized on that.

We also managed a lot of public offerings. I think we did sixteen of them. Often, I helped put them together, then I had to go around and sell them. I earned big payouts on those. Again, the other analysts were furious. Unfortunately, I did little to try to make peace.

An example: Personal computers were becoming necessary. Wheat bought eight or ten super Apple computers and put them in what used to be a conference room on the twelfth floor. Everybody had to book thirty-minute increments ahead of time to use those computers.

Sometimes we needed something done and we couldn't get the computers because they were all booked up. I went out and bought a couple myself. When we went out to buy them, instead of buying the super Apples, we went ahead and got the new 128s. That was like lighting another firecracker under everybody. Everybody got mad at us all over again because my assistant and I had computers. Oh, I was the only analyst with a full-time assistant, too.

So after several years—maybe four years—the firm got everybody Apple 128 computers. You know what we did? We upgraded to the new Macs, which made everybody mad at us again.

I would call on institutional accounts that held furniture stocks. Peter Lynch at Fidelity loved the furniture industry. They were one-decision stocks. You bought them when everybody hated the industry and housing looked terrible. Then you rode them until housing began to look good. By that time the stocks had gone up five, six-fold. That's when you bail out. I am mentioned in Lynch's first book as an analyst he could trust, which I thought was a huge compliment.

We built up a bit of a franchise. We got a lot of national coverage in *Fortune* and *Forbes*. We were in *The Wall Street Journal* regularly. Pretty soon after I joined Wheat, I was invited to the White House to talk about consumer spending on durables. How many analysts get invited to the White House? I was invited to go overseas to talk about the industry, and I went.

With all this, I was not generally liked at Wheat. I had my friends. But most people just endured me. I could point to my revenues, and I was bringing in cash fees, not commissions.

**It's hard for me to believe that people didn't like you personally.
Was it more professional envy?**

I hate to use the word *envy* because I can't imagine anybody en-
vying me about anything. I'm a very, very fortunate person to have gone
to good schools and found a job that I really enjoy. But when it comes to
competing, maybe I just never learned how to compete.

Let me give an example. For most analysts, their bonus was a very
slim percent of the retail brokers' commissions on their assigned stocks.
We had hundreds of retail brokers serving individuals in several states.
Our institutional sales team, about ten or twelve people, served large professional investors like bank trust departments, mutual funds, and others.
Our bonus from this department was determined by votes from the institutional salespersons.

The analysts and the institutional sales force met regularly, and
each analyst met with them one day a week, in the afternoon after the
market closed. Since there were about fifteen analysts, we met alone with
the institutional sales team about every three months. My stocks were
not often institutional favorites, so to help my presentation, I began to
take snacks. That got me votes.

The other analysts complained, so I was told not to take snacks.
Instead, I took meals like pizza or Sally Belle's box lunches. That got me
more votes and again made the other analysts angry. I was told to not take
meals, so I began to bring beer and wine. You can guess what happened.
Did all this make me popular? Not with anyone but the institutional sales
team.

Anyway, we built this practice doing acquisitions and public offerings. Jimm Mann joined me in 1978. We had as many as eight people
on the furniture team there for a while. Howard Armistead, Jimm's best
friend, came over to work specifically with me, and we became friends.
Jimm Mann had been promoted to head of Mergers and Acquisitions.

In 1988 or '89, Jim Wheat thought it was the right time to build a
building for Wheat, First Securities, not just rent space in another building. That was the birth of the Twin Towers downtown. The floors that
Scott & Stringfellow occupy today were originally Wheat's floors, designed
by the Wheat team. We moved there in December of 1990.

Why did you leave Wheat?

Around 1988, Wheat merged with Butcher Singer out of Philadelphia. That increased the firm size by 50 percent, but there never was any fit at all. They didn't like us; we didn't like them. It was very much a forced marriage. Butcher Singer was a wounded duck, and they thought by joining us, they could make it better.

Soon after, management sold 25 percent of the company to the Hartford Insurance Company. What was that all about? Well, it gave Jim Wheat some liquidity, and that's about it as far as I could tell. But all of a sudden you had new people around who we were supposed to kiss up to. It just never was a very relaxed, comfortable place to work. You always had this feeling there were people elsewhere making decisions about your future and what they were going to let you earn.

I put up with it because I had a franchise of sorts, a good lifestyle in Richmond near our families, and I got almost anything I wanted because of my revenues. Almost every year, I was given a very negative annual review by the research department head, Lou Hannen or Jack Pickler. There were complaints about my attitude, my lack of company reports, and not spending sufficient time with retail and institutional sales. What I was doing was bringing in and getting deals done, which was more profitable for the company, and me, too.

Every time I received a bad review, I told the department head to reconsider my review, remembering that I was putting more money in his pocket than all the other analysts combined. The department head got a percentage of my corporate finance deals. My reviews always came back better. I told them if they were that unhappy with me, I would leave. Fortunately, I had regular offers from several other regional brokerage firms who wanted my corporate finance contacts. Looking back, I was really a jerk.

In 1990, Ed Morrissett wanted to retire. Bill Coogan from Goldman Sachs was hired to head the corporate finance department. He cussed like a sailor, often in front of women. He was absolutely ruthless. He came to my office and said he didn't know me and I didn't know him, but I made money. He told me the problem with the firm was too much overhead. There was Jim Wheat and his cronies upstairs. The guys he went to college with. These former bank presidents who used to amount to something.

He said we're going to throw them out. We're going to have a coup, and we're going to throw all them out. He was going to make the company lean, and the people that really generated the commissions and really made the money would be the ones left. We'd run it, and we'd make a lot of money.

That struck me as wrong. First of all, this guy hadn't been around long enough to earn his stripes. Second, I told him I was uncomfortable even talking about this. We were in Jim Wheat's building. I worked for Jim Wheat. I wasn't going to talk about this. I wasn't going to have anything to do with it. He told me I was the first person to turn him down. I replied that he should just count me out. If he fired all them, he could fire me too. I wasn't worried about that. He said no, I'd be okay because I'm a producer. I wasn't overhead, like research. I was a producer.

The more I thought about it, the more upset I got. Jimm Mann and Coogan didn't get along well. All this was happening in November or December. And in January or early February 1991, everyone knew that Coogan and Jimm Mann were not getting along and could not work with each other, even though Jimm, as previously noted, was department head of the Mergers & Acquisitions Group. Jimm hadn't done anything wrong, but he was a staunch Jim Wheat loyalist and Jimm just wouldn't put up with a lot of Coogan's bull****". It was during this time that Jimm decided to leave Wheat and to form a new boutique merger and acquisition firm. It should be noted here that Jim Wheat, a VMI man who greatly valued loyalty, actually sent us a very small piece of business in the opening months of our start-up endeavor.

A week later, Howard left. They'd already rented the building next door to our current office. On April 1, 1991, when I received my paycheck and a large deal bonus, I sent sixty-some notes out to Wheat friends and two formal letters, resigning.

We started our own business in 1991. The three founding partners are all still here. We own our own real estate, all our equipment, and all our furnishings. We've done everything we can to minimize our overhead. We only have eight employees, and that's the way we want it. When we have a big year, everybody has a big year. When you've got this few employees, and you do a deal that's got a two-million-dollar finance fee on it, that goes a long way toward making everybody smile. So we don't tend to lose people. My assistant has been with me eleven years. I could not be more proud of him.

In 1992, the Furniture Manufacturer's Association named me their *Man of the Year.* I was elected into the American Furniture Hall of Fame in 2002. I am the youngest person ever to get in the Hall of Fame. When I was honored last June by the Anti-Defamation League at a dinner in New York City, I said in my speech, "There's a cartoon out there, a sign asking about a lost dog. The sign says, 'Lost three-legged dog with one eye, a broken tail, and answers to the name of Lucky.' " I said, "I feel very much like Lucky." I've got lots of problems. They're visible problems. But I married the right girl. I had the chance to go to great schools and get a great education. I joined a great firm. And to this day, I feel guilty that while Scott & Stringfellow paid for my education in the industry, Wheat, First Securities made all the money off of me.

I look back on my time in this industry, and I was so blessed to be where I was. To have the few contacts I had, to be able to leverage those, and then to have Jimm and Howard come into my life, and for the three of us to have enough confidence to start this. And do we fight? Yeah.

But we always end up doing what is right.

VII

MANAGEMENT

WILLIAM P. SCHUBMEHL

Before serving as president and chief executive officer of Scott & Stringfellow from 1992 through 1996, Bill was in charge of branch administration and retail sales. After stepping down as president, he retained his investment broker responsibilities until 2005. Bill has won numerous awards, but perhaps more impressive, has one named for him: Scott & Stringfellow's Schubmehl Award for Service Excellence.

In 1961, when I started in the investment business in Richmond, the Main Street area was a very exciting place to work. The corners of Ninth Street and Main Street were known as the financial crossroads of Virginia. There were national banks on each corner, and these offices were their Virginia headquarters. The banks were surrounded by brokerage firms and law firms. At that time, there were seven New York Stock Exchange member firms domiciled in Richmond, with their main offices on Main Street

I started my career at J. C. Wheat & Company, which was located at Tenth and Main in the American Bank Building. It was said to be one of the last buildings built on Main Street before the Great Depression of 1932. The Ross Building was built in 1965, which J. C. Wheat moved into in 1966. One indication of the closeness of the Main Street investment community, or my restlessness, was that during my fifty-year career on Main Street I was employed with J. C. Wheat, Branch, Cabell, Bank of Virginia, and Scott & Stringfellow (for thirty-five years). All of these firms were on the same block of Main Street.

You were there for Scott & Stringfellow's IPO.

I was there. As a matter of fact, I have the tombstone, which is the industry's term for the official announcement of the underwriting and the firms participating in the underwriting. It's interesting to look at the firms who underwrote the offering—I think there were twenty-five to thirty of them—and see how many are left. There aren't many.

You were also there for the sale to BB&T in 1999. Did the culture of Scott & Stringfellow change after the sale?

The culture didn't change because the players stayed—Buford Scott and Freddie Bocock were still in charge and always set high standards; John Sherman was the president, and things moved smoothly. BB&T also owned Craigie & Company, which was mainly a bond firm, and put Craigie together with Scott & Stringfellow. I think it was quite an adjustment for the people at Craigie to combine with a common stock-oriented firm. But our firm had experience in mergers, since we had already acquired Horner, Barksdale, a Lynchburg bond firm, and Investment Corp of Virginia, a NYSE firm located in Norfolk.

There is a different lifestyle at brokerage firms and banks. At a bank, you're trying to work your way up the ladder of success and get into management. As a broker, you're really dependent on how much you produce and how big your business is, because that's how you are compensated. Brokers are very independent, and it does take some adjustment between the two organizations.

Most firms were family owned and members of the New York Stock Exchange. There were J. C. Wheat & Company, Scott & Stringfellow, Davenport & Company, Branch & Company, Branch, Cabell & Company, Anderson & Strudwick, and a few others that I may have missed. They were all located on Main Street. Now, the only independent one left is Davenport. The others have been acquired by banks or merged with other national brokerage firms. Most Virginia banks were merged with other national banks, so there just aren't too many independent firms left on Main Street.

How did Scott & Stringfellow handle the Crash of 1987?

It came as a big surprise—to me, anyway. The market, as I remember, hit a high in August. Things were rolling along, and then all of a sudden interest rates started going up. As interest rates went up, the market started going down and computers began flashing *sell* signals.

I was on the executive committee at the time. We always had our meetings on Monday at lunch. People often said there would be a day when the market would drop over one hundred points. Until that Friday before, it hadn't happened.

So on Monday, the market was down something like one hundred points as lunch began. I came back from lunch and someone said it was down 150 points—but had been down 400 points earlier! I couldn't believe it. Then in the afternoon the market just started to really freefall. There was no buying whatsoever to support stock prices.

Investment funds managed by computers using *portfolio insurance* were selling indiscriminately. Trades were entered but the DOT[27] system backed up and orders were not being executed. We realized this the next day, but the market closed down five hundred points, and there was just no stability. But even with all the confusion, the market ended the year higher. It was nasty but short, compared to the 1973–74 bear market that slowly ground lower for two years.

There was another traumatic day in the market in 1962, a year after I started. The Dow was down thirty-two points and volume was something like thirteen million shares. There was a lot of drama, and it made a big impression on me.

In those days, all trades were printed and shown across the nation on the ticker tape. It was hard to get up-to-date stock prices then, so investors and spectators would gather at brokerage offices on Main Street to sit and watch the tape. You could have a large crowd of observers sitting in your office, particularly if it was an active down day. Every time a price would change, the Teleregister board, an electronic board which listed a hundred or so stock prices, would click. When the ticker tape ran five minutes late, an orange light would come on. And when it ran twenty or thirty minutes late, a red light would come on. It was an exciting environment, like a race track, as stock prices changed, the board clicked, and the lights changed from orange to red.

I think the tape was running an hour and a half late when the market closed that day, so you never knew what price you were receiving for purchases or sales. This unknown caused stress to traders, leading to even greater declines.

Why was the market down big that day? Were we just in the middle of a bear market or was there any news?

I think the market was due for a decline. John F. Kennedy was president at the time, and he was having a major dispute with steel company executives about raising prices. Conservative people didn't trust Kennedy in the first place. When a market's ready to go down, there's always an excuse for it.

Now, thirteen million shares these days is like the first trade of the day. In the break of '29, volume was twelve or thirteen million shares, and that wasn't really surpassed until Lyndon Johnson announced in 1968 that he was not going to run for president again. The market took off on the up side. And from 1968 on for a couple of years, we had tremendous volume. That led to a paperwork crunch.

Firms couldn't handle the paperwork because of the heavy volume. In those days, you actually moved stock certificates between buyers and sellers. It got to a point where in 1968 the market closed at 2:00 every afternoon to give firms a chance to catch up with the paperwork. Many never did catch up, and several firms went out of business. Abbott, Proctor & Paine, the biggest firm in Richmond at the time, had big problems trying to catch up. The back office had gotten so far behind that they were forced to sell offices and merge.

In your career, what have been some of the really great Richmond public companies?

One that comes to mind, an exciting company before it went out of business, was Best Products. Best Products had come up with a unique marketing and sales system. If you lived in the West End of Richmond, you went to Best Products. They went public, and as they say, it was a hot issue! Others that come to mind include Albemarle Paper, which appreciated sixfold after acquiring Ethyl Corp. CarMax was another successful idea and company. Markel has been a wonderful company and a great stock.

Whom did you succeed as president, and who succeeded you?

I succeeded Frank Pineno, who resigned to open a successful investment advisory firm. John Sherman, the manager of our Kinston, North

Carolina, office, succeeded me. When I became president, I talked to John about coming up and managing the branch system, which he eventually did.

When I started with Scott & Stringfellow, there were five branches. When I stepped down as president, there were something like twenty-five branches, give or take, because we had made a big move into North Carolina.

What's changed the most about the financial business?

The biggest change is technology! The Internet has changed our world in the last twenty years. I went to a meeting at the New York Stock Exchange twenty-five or thirty years ago, and they announced they were planning for one-hundred-million-share days. My thought was, you have got to be kidding.

There are seven or eight different locations where you can trade today and a billion shares, two, three billion shares a day is nothing. Commissions are virtually nothing now. That's a big change. Brokers and banks have merged and are competing vigorously in all types of financial services, including the money management business. Another change for the positive is the compensation system. Brokers as well as bankers are compensated based on assets under management, not just transactions.

Ninth and Main is not the financial crossroads of Virginia any longer, and if there is one, I am not sure where it is. The bank buildings are apartments, the private dining clubs are closed, and fast food and curbside lunch stands have taken their place.

Steve, a graduate of the Lawrenceville School and Tulane University, was executive vice president at Ferris, Baker Watts in Baltimore back when FBW would compete with similarly sized Richmond firms for investment banking business. Like several independent Richmond brokerage firms, FBW ultimately sold to a big bank. Says Steve: "Before the mid-1980s, capital markets existed, but the business was widely syndicated, handled by the five or six hundred members of the New York Stock Exchange. The average size firm might be fifty people or maybe even smaller, compared to today, where a handful of mega worldwide players control the business."

In the beginning of '94, George Ferris [28] fired Todd Parchman, and I boldly went forward and proposed that I run capital markets, along with two other colleagues. George thought that was a great idea. George was really big on building corporate capital markets, as he called it. He was pretty disillusioned with retail brokers for a whole variety of reasons . . . they always wanted more, more, more. Brokers were hard to deal with.

And they thought George was hard to deal with. Anyway, George and I quickly got to know each other, and I thought he was a completely reasonable person, which put me in the minority at Ferris, Baker Watts. But he and I thought alike, and George had institutional-type requirements, the way he did business. That was what I was used to.

In the early '90s we were coming out of a period of huge growth. Value stocks were no longer value stocks; they had appreciated from eight times earnings to fifteen times earnings. Growth stocks were in great demand. George wanted to participate in that in the worst possible way. He needed some Young Turks, so he was very interested in pitching the fact that Ferris, Baker Watts wanted to grow the business and was willing to put its money where its mouth was. And remember, it was in George's DNA to throw nickels around like manhole covers.

George was trying to make acquisitions. He had been in discussions with Buford Scott about merging Ferris, Baker Watts with Scott & Stringfellow to create something that would be along the lines of a Wheat First Butcher Singer kind of model. George thought Baltimore and Richmond were similar. One of his favorite lines was he made money the old-fashioned way—he inherited it.

We didn't merge with Scott & Stringfellow. I suspect they had no interest in this brash, former engineer from Washington, D.C. So we opened the Richmond branch and hired Gordon Miller, a former Alex Brown guy, who could be the Pied Piper for Richmond brokers. We hired retail stockbrokers and institutional salesmen to work out of the office.

What about the potential sale of Ferris, Baker in 2008 to BB&T that never happened?

BB&T had acquired Scott & Stringfellow, and they were very much on our short list of acquisition partners. Kelly King had just taken over, and he came in and made the pitch for why they wanted to buy Ferris, Baker Watts.

Sometime before that, we had an issue with a rogue broker that led to a settlement with the Securities and Exchange Commission and clients. It was well known. There was nothing for us to hide. In fact, we delayed the sale process until all that was in the rearview mirror. Still, BB&T walked away.

Who were your Richmond competitors?

We were similar size with Scott & Stringfellow and bigger than Davenport, Branch, Cabell, and Anderson & Strudwick. We competed with Scott & Stringfellow on a lot of Mid-Atlantic bank deals. We followed a lot of the same companies.

We were friendly competitors, but it was more a situation where we worked together. We would be either in a syndicate or in some cases co-manage a transaction. But there was a lot of *not-invented-here* thinking when we'd invite them to be a co-manager and they'd say no, whereas they would say yes to a Paine Webber or someone like that. I think they considered us to be not suitably big enough or sophisticated enough. ▪

GEORGE T. BASKERVILLE

After graduating from the University of Virginia, George entered the U.S. Coast Guard and graduated from OCS school. He joined Merrill Lynch in Norfolk in 1962, a month before leaving the service, and returned to his native Richmond in institutional sales for Merrill when they opened an office here in 1968. George was managing director of the firm's Virginia complex (Richmond, Charlottesville, and Roanoke) from 1983 through 1995. He retired in 2007 after a forty-five-year career with the Thundering Herd.

Does Merrill Lynch trace its origins to Richmond? Donald Regan, chairman of Merrill Lynch, gave a presentation where he said Merrill Lynch's roots indeed go back to 1820 in Richmond.[29] It may be tenuous, but that's part of Merrill's records. I brought it to the attention of the *Richmond Times-Dispatch*, and they wrote an article about it.[30]

The firm must have felt the Richmond origin was important, because they put it on a sign outside of their Washington, D.C., office. It makes sense, because if you were running a Merrill Lynch office in Washington, D.C., you would probably want to invoke a location more friendly and warm, like Richmond, Virginia, than Washington, D.C. But I don't think Merrill made much of it. I hadn't heard the story when I went to work for the firm.

How about your origins in the business?

I went to work in 1962 for Merrill Lynch in Norfolk, Merrill's only physical location in Virginia at the time. My dad said the brokerage business was a good place to make money, which sounded like a valid argument to me. I also interviewed with Ron Cain of Wheat, in the American Bank Building on Tenth Street. I don't think I talked to another firm in Richmond. If I decided to come to Richmond, I probably would've gone to work for Wheat. Merrill, at the time, was the biggest brokerage house in the country. Number two was probably Bache, and number three was Francis I. duPont.

I came back to Richmond five years later when Merrill opened an office in town and worked for Roger Fraley. Our first office was at Seventh and Franklin. We moved to the F&M Center from Seventh and Franklin, and then, when I was manager, to the Eighth & Main Building, into Hunton & Williams' former offices.

You were a manager of Merrill Lynch in Richmond, a firm that was very different from those headquartered here.

Merrill Lynch is organized around performance, competition, and progress. We do things in a different way; we always have. We were charged with establishing a position of dominance and prominence here, just as in other cities.

But the world in which Merrill operated in Richmond, Virginia, was distinctly different from the world in which we operated anywhere else. We were a different breed of cat in Richmond, a city that was, historically, the most unique brokerage and investment banking community in the country. You cannot overstate the unique characteristics of the market-place in Richmond, or the challenges that presents for a firm like Merrill. So, we never were a typical Merrill Lynch office, because the Richmond market is different.

How so?

The biggest difference was the number of New York Stock Exchange member firms based in Richmond. You couldn't find another city in the country with that many member firms, outside of New York. And those firms had no competition other than themselves; the wire houses (national brokerage firms) tended to compete just with other wire houses, not the local firms. Baltimore may have had some of the same dynamics as Richmond, but our Baltimore office had been there since time immemorial, and it was more like a typical Merrill Lynch office. Richmond was a tough nut to crack, no doubt about it. People certainly knew more about Branch, Cabell than they did about Merrill Lynch.

We competed effectively and did well, but we never dominated the market to the extent that we expected. When I was managing in 1982, for example, we'd been here for fifteen years. The local firms had been here forever. Everybody knew the founding partners. I would say Dean Witter had the same difficulties that we did. I would be willing to bet that Dean Witter's expectations were higher than what they actually achieved. If they weren't, then Dean Witter wasn't shooting high enough.

Eventually, the Richmond-based firms largely disappeared. The number of names that I was competing against in 1982 was far greater than it would be today. The competition is different. I always thought it would be a good idea to bring a Goldman Sachs here, but that hasn't been tried.

I don't know that the jury is fully in yet as to what the long-term future of the financial services industry will look like. In twenty years it's not going to look like it does now. It doesn't look today like it did twenty years ago. And the industry certainly doesn't look like it did before 1975, when fixed-rate commissions ended.

Deregulation of commission rates was a big story. When I started in this business, there was one commission rate for stock transactions, one commission book, and it was based on one hundred shares. You calculated what one hundred shares would cost you. If you traded a thousand shares, the commission was ten times that. No volume discount—none. That was the fixed rate, and every member of the New York Stock Exchange charged the same price.

I was given a piece of directed business shortly after I started, an order for one thousand shares of Corn Products and three thousand shares of Campbell Soup. Now those were two very unimaginative purchases, but it was a conservative-type investment account, and I didn't have anything to do with creating it. Somebody was nice enough to give me the business. The commissions were staggering. Multiples of thousands of dollars. I could not believe it.

The reason those rates were as high as they were is because members of the New York Stock Exchange would set commissions such that the least profitable member firm could make a profit on that level of commissions. So, if you were a profitable firm in that environment, the world was your oyster. That's where Merrill wanted to go. That was before commission rates were deregulated in 1975.

Merrill Lynch was a very strong and powerful and terrific organization. I cannot tell you how valuable and enjoyable and rewarding my experience was for forty-some years. But it wasn't Davenport or Scott & Stringfellow. I'm not saying one is better than the other, but they're different.

VIII

PINSTRIPES

MICHAEL J. ZELL

Michael Zell runs Nathan's, a preeminent men's custom clothier in Richmond. His father, Nathan Zell, started the business in 1936, one of eight clothiers within a two-block stretch of his original 724 East Main Street shop. Nathan's operated at that location, and only one other, on Main Street for seventy-five years. The business moved a few blocks away to Three James Center in 2011, where the distinctive neon sign remains in the front window.

The tides of change were all around me on Main Street. Buildings around me were being sold and converted to housing, like dominoes. Firms weren't renewing leases, and buildings were emptying. The center of gravity had shifted from Ninth and Main to Tenth and Cary.

Many of my customers—bankers, lawyers, brokers, and insurance people—are in the James Center, or within a couple of blocks, and they're more inclined to buy custom suits and shirts. I wanted to be near them, and the space was available. I had a buyer ready to buy my building, so the stars all lined up. Our former building at 828 East Main Street is now the home to Apple Hospitality REIT.

The move to casual dress certainly has changed our industry. Clothiers like us used to have full staffs of in-house tailors who grew up in the business, but no longer. All of that work is now sent out to contract tailors. Clothing today is measured and bought online, but self-measuring leads to mistakes. I've measured so many people in my career, I could do it blindfolded, if I had to, by feel and touch.

Brooks Brothers came down here some time ago to discuss partnering with us, with the idea that Nathan's would operate stand-alone, custom tailoring stores for them in areas outside of their bigger cities. The idea never got off the ground; I think they just wanted to learn as much about our business as they could, for free.

There's still a market for people who want top-quality, handmade suits, and that's why we're the last man standing when it comes to brick-and-mortar custom clothiers. ■

IX

RISK AND REWARD

K.C. HOWELL

K.C. is on the Executive Committee of the seventy-four-billion-dollar[31] *Virginia Retirement System, and oversees a team of twenty-two investment profession- als responsible for public equity, private equity, credit strategies and real assets. The job requires his head to be on a swivel at all times—monitoring all types of investments and strategies to ensure that retirement funds are there for 678,000 active members and beneficiaries. We met in K.C.'s Main Street office, where his CFA® charter hung on the wall. That was a reminder of the days in the early 1990s when we studied for the exams together.*

My job is Managing Director of Global Investments. I'm right below the CIO (chief investment officer) and above the program heads that run our strategies. They are the folks that do the hard work. I try to help them, develop them, advocate for them, and design procedures that make sure that we're doing things in a consistent manner. I help ensure we protect sensitive data and information and structure our accounts and legal agreements in ways that are beneficial to us. What I'm really doing is serving the folks that work for me. We're all on the same mission, and my goal is to create an environment that lets them maximize their talent here at VRS.

How did you get started in the business?

I graduated from Christopher Newport College with a business de- gree in May of 1991. I was working as a bank teller for Crestar at the time in Hampton and saw an opportunity here in Richmond at headquarters in the investment area, with their Capitoline Investment subsidiary. I came up and interviewed with Barton Peters in May 1991.

He was head of quantitative investing, equity investing at Capito- line. I knew some computer coding, so I had a slight edge. I got the job offer on a Friday and started on a Monday, in June 1991, working with

Barry Ferguson and Barton Peters. Frank Atkins, Pete Brailey and Stuart Davies were also part of the research team when I joined.

It was an interesting time. You may remember that the Gulf War had just ended in the early winter of 1991. We were still benefiting from the peace dividend from the fall of the Soviet Union, and the Gulf War was a quick and decisive win. The markets were doing well. But banks were still struggling with some prior lending problems. There was some turnover at Capitoline, and that created opportunities for me to take on more responsibilities.

I worked with Erwin Will, CIO at the time. I've known him for twenty-six years, and he's taught me a lot through various types of engagements. He founded Capitoline in 1972 and was a great leader with an easygoing way. I still follow his lead. He taught me that hiring people smarter than I am was a good strategy.

Jeff Markunas came over from Sovran Bank in 1992 to join Crestar Asset Management, which by then had changed its name from Capitoline. Lane DeCost and Lyn Swallen joined him shortly thereafter. They took me to a different level as an analyst and a portfolio manager. Jeff gave me a lot of opportunities, and I'm forever grateful for that.

I also started the CFA program in 1992 and was married the same year. By 1993 I was a research analyst writing research reports, old school fundamental research. As we rolled into 1994, David Halloran, who was running a mutual fund that I had been working with, departed, and I took over the fund. That was my beginning on the money management side.

So, stock research analyst, then analyst plus equity mutual fund manager . . . just more opportunities. My first child was born in August 1995, and I received notification that I'd passed the CFA Level III exam the same week. It was a great week.

What kind of mutual fund did you manage?

It was a growth mutual fund, large cap. I brought in some size discipline, versus just being equal weighted. I was conscious of that type of benchmarking. I ran it for three years, and it did fine.

My involvement in the Richmond Society of Financial Analysts led me to work with Nancy Everett, who was on the board with me. In 1998, Nancy started to talk to me about opportunities she had at the Virginia

Retirement System. She's really a wonderful individual. She's currently at VCU. She left VRS in '05 to run General Motors' pension fund in New York City, then went to BlackRock for a while, and has come back to Richmond.

I didn't have any inside information, but I knew Crestar's independence was in question. I remember distinctly an all-staff meeting where one exercise was a board game called The Play, where you faced various challenges. Think of The Game of Life, where you have successes and move forward, or reversals and move back. One of the challenge scenarios we needed to overcome in order for the bank to remain independent was to achieve an 18 percent return on equity. And from my analytical experience, I thought, wait a minute, hold on. They're sending us a signal, right?

I sensed something was coming and started to entertain other ideas, because I didn't want to relocate. Nancy made an offer to me in April 1998. SunTrust announced the acquisition of Crestar in July 1998. I was lucky, but the writing had been on the wall. There was a lot of bank consolidation going on, and it was just a matter of time.

In 1998, we were about to experience a market melt-up scenario. Technology was changing the way we did everything. Computing power enabled us to do a lot more interesting things. The productivity gains that we saw were pretty dramatic.

The democratization of financial data was really starting to take off. Financial people in the business no longer held the cards and notified the public about what the markets did. The public had their own news sources and opinions. *The Wall Street Journal* was online. Financial advisors would have clients who saw something on CNBC or one of the twenty-four-hour finance channels, and they wanted an answer about what was going on in the market or that stock. Clients sometimes were ahead of the breaking news. That democratization of data has just not stopped. We see it in all parts of our life right now.

I worked at VRS for a few years, and in 2000 I made a decision to focus exclusively on the external management of assets. My coworker, J.T. Grier, has a strong econometric skillset and is a self-taught coder. We were very risk-controlled and have found success in quantitative active management.

So you were in charge of VRS' external managers.

Yes. VRS has a long history of innovation in outside managers. We had private equity in '88 or '89. International investments in '89. Emerging markets in '94. Long/short equity in at least 1990. I inherited a very innovative basket of managers that Bob Hill, J.T., and others had helped set up. We just continued that process of innovation and looking for different strategies.

We viewed long/short investing as the way to maximize active management, because you're not limited by what we call the long-only constraint. That is, if you had a stock in the S&P 500 that was twenty basis points of exposure, one-fifth of a percent, and you hated it and thought it was going to zero, your option was to just not own it. But when you can short that bad stock, you can size your underweight to suit your risk tolerance (e.g., a 2 percent short position in the portfolio would equate to an underweight position of 220 basis points), instead of simply not owning the stock and having a twenty basis point underweight position. We do that only through externally managed assets. It will amplify your skills, and you better have the skills; otherwise, you're going to get in a lot of trouble.

I started running the global equity program. J.T. ran the internal effort, which represented approximately one-third of our public equity exposure.

What do market declines mean for the fund?

An imbalance between our assets and liabilities can cause an increase in the contribution rate, how much the taxpayers have to pay. We're focused on the beneficiaries of the plan—the teachers, the firemen, the state workers. Those beneficiaries are our main client. We also have to be mindful of the market's volatility, our fund's volatility on the state budget, because that contribution rate directly impacts the state budget.

So we have to balance eating well—i.e. high returns—with sleeping well, having relatively stable contributions. If they're too stable, we won't get the needed return. If they're too volatile, none of us are going to sleep well at night.

How do you feel about active versus passive management?

We're about 98 percent active. We believe in active management. But we think that there are smart ways to implement active management, and there are not-so-smart ways to implement active management.

We view active management fees as investments in excess return. So you have to have demonstrated competency in producing excess returns. Also, we're willing to pursue different types of risk premia or style premia to gain excess returns. Take private equity, for instance. We know that opportunities exist there because of illiquidity premiums and the control premiums.

When we evaluate managers, we consider not only performance, but philosophy. We want to intimately understand the culture of the organization. Favorable attributes include a strong culture, skin in the game, and low personnel turnover. Those characteristics tend to be ones that show a little more promise.

We look for replicable approaches. We don't want to see the gains all in one sector or one type of stock, for instance. And we want the rationale behind the gains to be founded in sound economic or behavioral approaches. The *I had a feeling about this stock* approach would not fly.

I think there's a place for fundamental active management. I think there's a place for quantitative active management. I think there's a place for long/short strategies in addition to long-only strategies. I think there's a place for higher-fee active management as long as you're getting paid for it.

Do you have to be mindful of any political considerations?

We've been an independent state agency since 1994. Does it get political? I would say not really.

The board delegates a lot of investment decisions to Ron Schmitz, our CIO, and the staff. They decide policy, how much is allocated to equities, how much is allocated to private equity, fixed income, etc. We execute the mission, as they define it, subject to risk controls. It is a very pure investment environment. It's not marketing. It's not dealing with multiple clients. We have one client with seventy-four billion dollars, as of June 2017.

Any closing comment?

The Virginia Retirement System accomplishes good things for the Commonwealth. And that means a lot to us. There's compensation, and there's title, and all of those things. But we go home at night knowing that we're doing everything we can to make sure that the plan is being managed the best way possible for the beneficiaries. ▪

Nancy is chief executive officer and chief investment officer of VCU Investment Management Company, providing investment services to Virginia Commonwealth University and its affiliates. Prior to VCIMCO, she spent three years as head of U.S. fiduciary management at BlackRock, five years as chief investment officer of the General Motors pension fund, and twenty-six years with the Virginia Retirement System, including seven as chief investment officer. It's fair to say that Nancy's insights into risk management of complex pension plan assets and liabilities have led to higher returns, with lower risk, for hundreds of thousands of retirees. We met in her Uptown office.

'm a proud graduate of VCU. I planned to be a lawyer and went to work for a law firm after graduating in 1979. I quickly decided I did not want to be a lawyer. I noticed a help-wanted ad in the *Richmond Times-Dispatch* for an accountant who'd be willing to learn computer programming. Computer programming was the hottest thing in 1979, and I had a BS in accounting, so I applied for the position, which was with the investment department of the Virginia Retirement System. I knew nothing about the business then. I landed the job and taught myself how to program in Fortran IV.

The retirement system ran a very large bond portfolio, and I wrote the program to account for our internal bond trading. The VRS had been allowed to invest only in bonds up until the mid-1970s, but a legislative change allowed investment in equities, so we had a small percentage of the portfolio in equities. A significant portion of the money had been invested in municipal bonds, which of course makes no sense today, because why would a tax-exempt entity invest in tax-exempt bonds? The rationale was that they paid reasonable rates, and it made sense for an agency of the Commonwealth to own the Commonwealth's debt.

So the Virginia Retirement System was exclusively invested in fixed income for much of the 1970s?

Yes, the Code of Virginia previously excluded equity investments, but things were changing. The VRS and the General Assembly and policymakers recognized that the retirement system was of major importance not only to state employees, but to the budget of the Commonwealth of Virginia, which turned out to be painfully true. You can look at history and see how the funding of the retirement system has become such a big issue with the state budget.

The Virginia Retirement System, having just been permitted to invest in equities, ran a portion of its equity portfolio internally, quite successfully. There was an *earnings momentum* philosophy back then, before the phrase even existed. There were maybe five people in the whole department. And the guys—of course, they were all guys—asked me to develop a computer program to help them pick stocks, which I did. Think about it: we were a public pension fund in Richmond, Virginia, in 1980, doing quantitative investing, which didn't become mainstream for another six or seven years.

We had a factor model, and I built a database. I can't remember what universe we used, but we were populating it with the P/E ratios and Value Line timeliness scores and other factors, which were used to pick stocks.

Being in the vanguard was the mantra at the VRS. Back then, if you were first, or early, in areas like international investing or private equity, you could take advantage of market inefficiencies.

VRS developed probably the most well-thought-out governance structure among public plans, following a massive uproar in the early '90s, when the retirement system bought the RF&P railroad. Formerly, most new governors appointed a new board of trustees every four years, so there was constant turnover. Now, instead, half of the board appointees were appointed by the General Assembly, with certain required qualifications, including investment experience for a couple of them, and term limits were instituted. The chief investment officer was hired by contract. Internally, we changed the decision-making structure, pushing decision-making down to the staff, with investment committee oversight, and policy set at the board level.

Suddenly, it became much easier to accomplish some of the things we wanted to do. At plans such as CalPERS, CalSTRS,[32] and others, no decision could be taken until a committee approved it. If your committee met quarterly, and you decided the market was overvalued and you needed to put a hedge on two days after the last meeting, your hands were tied.

VRS was early in thinking about not only the best way to invest, but the best way to govern, and how to attract the best and the brightest. Alice Handy, who at the time was the Treasurer of the Commonwealth and had run UVA's endowment, was on the investment committee. So were Buford Scott, Mark Finn, and Bobby Butcher, among many other astute investors. We had a group of investment professionals who brought interesting ideas to the table, and we had the ability to act on those ideas. For instance, when the real estate market crashed in 1990, we set up special purpose corporations to buy real estate, and made a lot of money doing it. We could do these types of things in a public pension fund, which was unusual, because we had the right governance structure and were able to bring the right people on board.

So I was lucky. I was a programmer, just going along for the ride. And then I thought, those investment guys are having a lot more fun, and they're making a lot more money, than I was. I want to be one of them. So I took and passed the CFA® exam, which was the only way I could achieve credibility back then. I started out managing an equal-weighted S&P 500 portfolio, which is exactly what it sounds like.

Before the changes in 1994, there was still some political turmoil at the VRS, and around 1990, all the senior people left except a couple of other people and me. I was told I was going to run the bond portfolio, even though I didn't really know much about bonds. So I did that, and continued to become involved in a lot of other different areas. By the mid '90s, I decided I wanted to be the chief investment officer. I had the experience to do it. I had touched all the asset classes and had worked on developing asset allocation.

People would ask me why I stayed at a public pension fund all those years. It was the best place in the world. We had billions of dollars of assets. I remember calling Bill Sharpe after he won the Nobel Prize, because he was our consultant. It was crazy stuff, and I was just a kid. But I was given the opportunity to grow. I became the deputy chief investment officer and then chief investment officer.

What type of asset classes did the VRS adopt when you were there?

I was responsible for international equity investing in the early '80s, which was very, very difficult back then. In order to travel overseas, we had to get the governor's approval. We did other asset classes, like long/short investing and managed futures. I helped John McLaren put that program together. We did real estate and private equity. We hired Charles Grant, a bond guy, who became chief investment officer. Charles was a very smart investor. Every once in a while he would come in my office with an idea that could make a lot of money, like TIPS,[33] a trade he identified one time that was so good it theoretically was never supposed to happen.

One of the things I was very proud of was trustee training. If you were appointed to the board of the VRS, sooner or later a reporter would stick a microphone in your face and ask why the portfolio was down billions of dollars, as it was in the Crash of 1987. That may just be a small percentage of the total fund, but the article wouldn't mention that, just the billions of dollars. And some poor teacher from XYZ County would have to defend that.

We trained the trustees to understand what we were doing. Even though they weren't investment people, they understood that we were long-term investors. That helped us to move forward where others couldn't, because a lot of funds are run by boards and committees that are so reactive. We trained ours to not be reactive, to really think long term. It's not about getting into the minutiae of do we own this stock or that stock. At the board level, it's about understanding the policy, why the policy exists, how it's determined, and importantly, how you're not going to change it just because the situation changes in the short term.

One time Gene Cox, the local TV reporter, came to see us after some event—I can't recall which one—caused a steep market decline. He remarked that things seemed so calm in our offices, and he was a little surprised that we weren't more frantic. What we *were* doing was examining where we stood and deciding what we should be buying. We followed a very measured and thoughtful process.

Why did you decide to leave?

Alice Handy had started Investure, a third-party, outsourced chief investment officer (CIO) firm in Charlottesville. She was an early mover in the outsourced CIO industry. I thought the idea was a great one, and we talked. Alice suggested I talk to Allen Reed, who ran the General Motors pension fund. GM, as it started its descent, had spun off several subsidiaries, such as Delphi and Hughes. Because it was so complicated to figure out how to divvy up $120 billion in those trusts, the decision was made to have the General Motors pension fund group run them all.

Presto change-o, Allen was in the third-party outsourcing business, which he grew further by taking on Xerox.

I called Allen to pick his brain and had lunch with him in New York. He said the outsourced CIO idea was interesting, but that he had a better idea. He was getting ready to retire and suggested I put my hat in the ring for his job. That's how I got the General Motors position. I commuted to New York for those years, and then went to BlackRock.[34]

You were there when GM filed for bankruptcy. How did that affect you?

It was crazy. Not only was GM filing for bankruptcy, but the markets were melting down in crisis. So I had a double-edged sword. When I arrived, we were about 40 percent hedged, which meant about 40 percent of the assets were exposed to the long bond. We actually took that up another 10 or 20 percent right before the market meltdown. We made tons of money. Dumb luck. We weren't making an interest rate bet. We were simply hedging the portfolio against liability volatility.

The pay czar[35] wanted to know the top twenty highest-paid people at GM, and my people and I were on the list. So we got involved in those headlines, which was difficult. But from an investment perspective, the General Motors pension fund was in pretty good shape. That went really well, but the turmoil was not pleasant.

When I took the job, I became part of senior management. Every quarter I would fly to Detroit and sit with senior management and listen to how they were dealing with events. That's another book. It was a very fascinating period to watch people who had literally grown up at GM. That's how you did it. You started in the Treasurer's Office in New York. If you did well, you ran Europe or you ran Korea. If you were very, very successful, you ended back in Detroit in senior management.

Financially, senior management was very astute because almost everyone had a finance background. There are a bunch of reasons why GM went bankrupt, but the pension fund was not one of them.

I'll tell this story. We were one of the largest investors in the Capital International Emerging Market Growth Fund, so I was on the board. We held our annual meetings once a year in an emerging market, and it was in Vietnam in 2008. The meeting happened to be the week that Lehman went bankrupt.[36] The time difference in Vietnam is twelve hours. The

GM issue is bubbling. I'm in Vietnam. Lehman is going bankrupt. I'm up all night dealing with the people in New York and talking to the banks and trying to figure out what's going on with Morgan Stanley, etc., and I'm up all day going to Capital International meetings. And finally, after two days, I said I've got to go back. I can't get any sleep because I'm working 24/7.

Things were pretty stable in the New York office, as the only functions left were the pension fund and the treasury. Turnover increased after the bankruptcy filing in 2009 and the government stepped in and fired Rick Wagoner[37] and Fritz Henderson[38] and others, and brought in outside people.

We had a small, profitable third-party chief investment officer business. But my little business wasn't going to make a dent in GM's issues, so they decided to shut it down. That's when I decided to leave, after five years.

I left GM in the spring of 2010 and came back to Richmond. I ride horses, and I was having a tremendous time. By the time winter came, I became a little restless. My husband Rob asked what I was going to do, and I didn't know. I wasn't ready to retire.

Larry Fink, the chairman of BlackRock, called me and asked what I was up to. When I told him not much, he invited me to come to New York to talk.

I became enamored with BlackRock. You know, I've run an asset management firm within a public pension fund, and that brought its own peculiar challenges. And then I ran an asset management firm within a failing manufacturing company, and that had a lot of issues. Wouldn't it make sense to run one inside of an asset management firm, where I wouldn't be off to the side?

Of course, I had to pick the largest one in the world. The dynamics of trying to be meaningful inside BlackRock are quite challenging. To put BlackRock's size in perspective, they have to create the functional equivalent of something like a three-hundred-million-dollar asset management firm *every year* just to continue historical profit and margin trends. It's a very successful firm and has made a lot of smart moves. I think the smartest move—and they probably would admit it—is buying iShares and becoming part of the unbelievable wave of success in the ETF front.

I stayed at BlackRock for three years before the weekly commute just became too much. Rob said I should come on home to Richmond, which I did. I was on VCU's Board of Visitors, and now I'm here with VCIMCO.

How many employees do you have at VCIMCO?

We have eight. William Lee, the COO, worked with Summit Rock Advisors in New York, a very successful third-party asset management firm. He had the great good sight to marry a woman from Richmond. A couple of years ago, they decided they'd rather raise their kids in Richmond. He brought in Phil Keefe, who was at Bain Capital and Cambridge Associates. We brought in Bruce MacDonald, who had been at University of Virginia Investment Management Company. Maggie Millhiser had been at Investure. We have an analyst and the operations support group. We're all generalists, not specialists. We observe what's going on in the world to help us decide why we should have X, Y, or Z in the portfolio. It seems to work quite well.

How much do you manage today?

It's a little over a billion dollars, with another billion available from within the VCU system. When Mike Rao[39] said VCU should start its own investment management company, I thought assets would be something like two hundred million. The actual number was close to two billion. I thought, two billion? Where did VCU get two billion?

It's not all endowment money. A big slug of that is very, very long-term operating capital for VCU and the health system. And the balance comes from the endowments for VCU's various programs, such as Engineering.

It's January 2018. Stocks say blue skies ahead for the economy, while interest rates say the opposite. How do you reconcile that? What do you do as a steward of a billion dollars?

Starting VCIMCO is very unique. Now VCU and its affiliates have a dedicated team with a true long-term focus. We are building a portfolio that will meet the needs of VCU far into the future. You have to take a long-term view. If you react to short-term phenomena, you're putting things at risk. When we started two years ago in October, we thought the equity markets were pretty richly valued. But we couldn't take the risk of being out of the market.

We put most of the money in passive ETFs. We struck our asset allocation and determined that we needed to earn a 5 to 6 percent real return. That's really hard to do in the markets we have right now. It's very difficult to figure out how you're going to get there from here.

We knew we had to employ active strategies, and we knew over the long term we had to hold a higher equity exposure because you're certainly not going to be able to get that kind of real return in a fixed income portfolio. We struck the portfolio in short-dated treasuries, because we didn't like the long end of the bond market, and global passive equity. We then began by hiring long/short managers because we want protection on the down side, when the inevitable happens.

We've also introduced a certain amount of volatility hedging, which is unbelievably cheap today. We're willing to give up twenty-five, thirty, maybe fifty basis points of premium for the protection. It's cheap, and if the markets crack, the payoff is huge.

So you take measures like that, but you can't fret about valuation because markets can run for long periods of time. The right thing to do is to pick what you're going to do and stick with it. That's what we did at the VRS. I don't know what the market's going to do. How does anyone know in the short term?

What I'm confident of in the long term is that the market will correct and return to something normal. You have had ten years of monetary intervention that has to work its way out of the system.

If I have anything that I would regret over the years it's been the rare periods when something was obvious and we didn't act. In 2001, 2002, you may have been early, but you would've been right if you hedged some of your technology exposure.

[*At this point I asked Nancy if the GM pension plan's move to sell stocks and buy bonds in 2006 and 2007 wasn't the market call of a career. That decision steered the plan away from the perfect storm of dramatically lower stock prices and lower interest rates in the following years. Nancy says it wasn't a market call on her part, just a hedge. She's modest. I'll note that in 2008, GM's pension fund outperformed a peer group by eight hundred basis points* [40]—*a Babe Ruth-level accomplishment in the pension world. Ed.*]

I don't give personal advice, but once in a while someone will ask what they should do with their 401(k). My reply is to rip up your statements. Just don't read them. You will be tempted to make a poor decision if you do.

You've worked in New York for the biggest asset manager in the world and one of the largest car companies in the world. But you've never left Richmond. Please tell me about that.

I love Richmond. When I worked at a law firm as a bookkeeper in the early '70s, one of my jobs was to make individual bank deposits for the partners. So at lunch once or twice a week, I would walk downtown and go to F&M, and Central Fidelity, and the buildings and architecture were gorgeous. I'd go to Miller & Rhoads for lunch, and the ladies would be drinking tea with their gloves on. I loved it. My sisters were mortified. They're both lawyers in New York City, and they thought I must have read too many romance novels.

What do I do? My biggest passion is riding horses, which you can't do in a lot of cities. But I board my horses in Richmond, a thirty-minute drive from my house.

I grew up in a very small town near Ithaca, New York. I never wanted to live in New York City. It was just too big. GM's office was at Fifty-ninth and Fifth, right on Central Park. Some of my colleagues thought their commute was easy—it was only an hour and ten minutes each way. Here in Richmond, some people would complain if it took fifteen minutes to get to work. I'd say to the guys at GM, you want quality of life? Move to Richmond.

Central National Bank Building. The Art Deco skyscraper
on Broad Street was completed in 1929.

Freddie Bocock, Frank Pineno, and Buford Scott,
pictured in Scott & Stringfellow Financial's
debut 1987 annual shareholders' report.

Customers watching the tape
in Scott & Stringfellow's board
room, October 19, 1989.

Main Street skyline, October 1986: United Virginia Bank,
Sovran Center, Omni Hotel, and Dominion Bank.

The Ironfronts, built in 1866, a year
after Richmond burned; former home to
Branch & Co. and Branch, Cabell & Co.

License plate on Willie Walters' new 1987
Chrysler LeBaron. "I'll trade anything *for an
eighth.*"

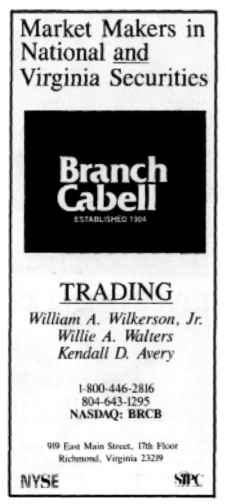

Branch, Cabell
ad in *Traders
Magazine,*
August, 1988.

Ron Moody and the Centaurs
opened for The Showmen
at Tantilla in 1968. A local
stockbroker handled the booking.

The "NOW concept in Investment Banking"? Ad from the 1970s.
Mason-Hagan merged with Fidelity Corp. in 1970. Fidelity
acquired Craigie in 1972, forming Craigie, Mason-Hagan, Inc.

L. P. King, Stafford White, Johnny Moran, Jim White, and Con Shea. Circa 1985.

Richmond-based Eskimo Pie Corp. was spun off from Reynolds Metals in 1992. EPIE is now part of Nestlé.

Virginia Trust Company Building, 821 East Main Street, built in 1919. The trust company merged with Virginia National Bank in 1973.

Board-boy chalking quotes at the Jefferson Hotel boardroom of Shoaf & Shoaf, Inc., an investment firm, late 1920s.

IN MEMORIAM

The employees of Anderson & Strudwick, Inc. would like to extend our condolences on the passing of Mr. James C. Wheat, Jr., the former Chairman of Wheat First Securities, Inc.

It is our belief that James C. Wheat, Jr. was the most capable and effective Virginia investment banker of his time. Through his efforts, countless Virginia businesses were financed, thousands of jobs were both created and sustained. He was and always will remain an inspiration to all of us in the brokerage business.

Charlie A. Mills, III	Chairman of the Board, Senior Vice President	Thomas C. Robertson	President
George W. Anderson	Senior Vice President	L. McCarthy Downs, III	Senior Vice President
Peter C. Einselen	Senior Vice President	John V. Garland	Senior Vice President
J. Douglas Gordon, Jr.	Senior Vice President	James W. Grove	Senior Vice President
Paul W. Mehaffey	Senior Vice President	Donald H. Newlin	Senior Vice President
James H. Bailey	Vice President	David S. Ellington	Vice President
George S. Jones	Vice President	William S. Luck	Vice President
James C. Miller	Vice President	Jean S. Schwindt	Vice President
Michael M. Via	Vice President	G. Lee Wilkinson, Jr.	Vice President

Anderson & Strudwick condolences on the passing of Jim Wheat in the *Richmond Times-Dispatch,* May 5, 1992.

Richmond's Federal Reserve Bank was located on Capitol Square from 1922 to 1978, top. The new Fed building on Byrd Street, designed by the same architect who designed the World Trade Center, was completed in 1978.

X

COMPOUNDING MACHINE

THOMAS S. GAYNER

Tom is co-chief executive officer of Markel Corp., which includes managing its twenty-five-billion-dollar investment portfolio. Professional money manager peers regard him as one of the best in the business, and if you're a Markel shareholder, you know that. I visited Tom in his unpretentious West End office, sitting across a wall with a framed Wall Street Journal *article on one end and Nascar wall art on the other.*

Technically, I started in the business in 1984, when I went to Davenport. But it's probably worthwhile to go back a bit to figure out how that came about.

Remember the TV show *Green Acres*? I would say my father was halfway between Mr. Douglas and Mr. Haney. He was an accountant in Philadelphia with the predecessor firm of Deloitte. His family had a substantial business that went bankrupt during the Depression, so times were pretty meager and lean. He ended up attending a junior college in Illinois. I don't know exactly how he found the place, but at that time tuition, room, and board, all in, was twenty-five dollars a year. Even then, that was a good deal.

It was Blackburn College, a work college, and it still exists today with the same sort of program. Tuition, room, and board might be ten or twenty thousand, something like that, which is a deal for a private school today. The reason for the low cost, as my father said, was that other than the faculty, there were only two professionals on the staff: the president of the college and the head of maintenance. The students themselves cut the grass, did the cooking, and the plumbing. They raised animals for food. Painting and electrical work, plumbing, the whole nine yards—all of that was done by student labor to keep the place going. It was a very affordable way to get an education.

Dad was drafted in World War II as an infantryman, lowest of the low, base-level private in the Army. He served in the Seventh Army and earned the Purple Heart. He came home and received an accounting degree from Temple on the G.I. Bill.

He became a CPA and worked for a firm in Philadelphia. He developed some business interests of his own outside of the firm, sleeping four hours a night and working all the time. By the time I was born in 1961, my father had left big city accounting and opened an accounting office in rural Salem, New Jersey. He became the first CPA ever in Salem County.

When I came along, he owned a liquor store and a tax practice. He would do real estate deals, small business deals, and workouts for bankruptcy judges, all from his office that was attached to our home.

So I grew up around business, and people working on tough problems, paying taxes, and trying to put deals together and build relationships. I loved my father. We had a great relationship. Every day after school, I would go and sit in his office, and I would do my homework. I would hear him talk to people and hear him talk on the phone and just absorb stuff. He read *The Wall Street Journal*, so I read *The Wall Street Journal*. You know the way you adore your father. Some kids talk about sports with their dads. We did that, too, but we also talked about business a lot. It was just a way that we connected.

He always had an active interest in the stock market, investments, and things of that nature. It was just part of the normal conversation. So when you ask when I started, I can never remember not being interested or curious or connected or involved in business and the stock market. I think I bought my first stock when I was in eighth grade. I'd never not owned a stock.

I went away to the Lawrenceville School and then the University of Virginia, where I received a degree in accounting (because that's what my dad did). It seemed like fun. I got my CPA license and thought I'd do a tour of duty in the world of large accounting firms. In those days you had to take the exam and then wait two years before you got your CPA license. Even if you'd passed the exam, you didn't get to call yourself a CPA until you had done your two-year apprenticeship.

In the back of my mind I thought, well, if that doesn't work or I don't like it or have fun, I'll just go work with my dad and carry on for him. Sadly enough, right when I was about to graduate from the University of Virginia, my father died of a heart attack A complete, epic surprise.

I did not see that coming at all. You kind of grow up in a hurry when that happens. That changes everything.

Fortunately, I had a job lined up with Coopers & Lybrand, as it was known at the time, one of the Big Eight firms. But the option of going back and working for my dad was gone. His clients needed to file tax returns right then, and I was in no position to help them do that. I had a degree from college, but zero experience. I helped my mother make arrangements to have another accountant take over his practice, because that's what needed to be done.

So I went to work for Coopers, in Richmond. I had looked in Philadelphia and Nashville, Tennessee, because I'd gotten married by then, and my wife's family was from Nashville. But I came to Richmond mainly because I'd loved UVA so much. I had such a great experience in Charlottesville, made a lot of friends, and liked Virginia.

This was 1983. Interest rates were just beginning to nudge down from their peak of 20 percent.

I really liked the people at Coopers and made some lifelong friends. It was a pretty natural transition from UVA, being a member of the Beta House; we were still just kids. Now we had work to do, an expense account, and business demands. We were working hard, but we were laughing and enjoying ourselves and having a lot of fun.

Along the way, as a hobby, I had been involved in the markets. After the course of a year and a half, there were some months where I was making more money from investments than I was as an accountant. I came to know Mike Beall at Davenport here in Richmond, who also had been with Coopers & Lybrand. He also liked investments more than accounting. Mike became my broker. He was also a research analyst and wrote reports for the firm.

One day Mike said, "People here at Davenport are kind of impressed with the way you're handling your account. How'd you like to come over here and work with me and do what I do in terms of becoming a broker and being an analyst?"

I said, "Well, that sounds like fun. I've got six more months until I hit my two-year mark on the CPA license. Would six months from now work?"

He said, "Well, they were hoping now."

I thought, yes, now is good. So I jumped to Davenport. That was

1984. I went to work with Mike, and we worked for Joe Antrim, who was the head of the research department. I got to know all kinds of supremely wonderful people. There were great teachers, great role models, and great mentors at Davenport. I was there through 1990.

In 1984 *Fortune* magazine published an article by Carol Loomis about Warren Buffett and Berkshire Hathaway. I remember reading that article and the scales just falling from my eyes. Every single word dripped with commonsense.

So I went into Joe Antrim's office, and said, "Hey Joe, have you ever heard of this guy named Warren *Bu-fay*?"

He said, "It's *Buff-ett*, you idiot," and just threw me out. Joe was a tough taskmaster in many ways. I went to the cutting-edge technology of the day, the S&P tear sheets. Berkshire was about $1,000 a share; that's the "A" stock, which is now $250,000 or so.

And like a twenty-three-year-old idiot, I thought to myself, no stock could possibly be worth a thousand dollars a share. To my everlasting regret, I did not buy it. But I became aware of Berkshire. I was enough of an accountant to look at the numbers and think they are pretty good. There is a compelling business being built here, so I kept following the company.

In 1986, Markel Corporation went public. At the time, Markel had a couple of different businesses but was predominantly insurance-based. They had an insurance underwriting operation, as well as claims handling and insurance brokerage. Markel was profitable from an underwriting point of view. Steve Markel,[41] the architect of the financial structure at Markel, had demonstrated that he was willing to invest in equity securities, which was pretty darn unusual. And it still remains the case today. A single-digit number of insurance companies use their underwriting profits to invest in long-term equity ownership positions.

Davenport happened to be a member of the underwriting syndicate, so I was exposed to the company and became the analyst covering Markel on behalf of Davenport. I saw the same architectural structure in place by which Buffett had built Berkshire. Those bones existed at Markel.

I liked the people, and bought some stock. From '86 through '90, I got to know Steve Markel, and he got to know me. He became a client and a friend. In 1990, Markel did a deal where it bought a company that was bigger than itself, more than doubling the size of the company. Steve had been handling investments by himself and thought he might like a partner to help him. He asked me to come here, and I thought, *Great!* I'd probably spent four years begging for the job beforehand because I saw what could happen.

Well here I am, twenty-eight years old, and I think that I can be part of building the next Berkshire. And it happens to be right here in Richmond, Virginia, where I live. The stock was eight dollars a share at that time (now it's a little bit more than that). When I walked in the door, Steve gave me two million dollars to manage. That doesn't sound like very much, but I'll remind you, the total assets of the company at that time were on the order of maybe sixty million. So it was a meaningful amount of money.

Within six months he kept pushing more and more responsibility to me. I don't remember the dates, but ultimately I became in charge of all equity investments, and then I became in charge of all investments, both equity and fixed income. Today that number stands at twenty-five billion or so. It's grown and done well.

Are you still hands-on when it comes to picking equities?

Yes. In fact, for the first seventeen or eighteen years I was here, I was a one-man department. We went from two million dollars under management to two billion at least, maybe more, with just me managing the equities. It was only seven or eight years ago that I finally added one person to the team. So now it's just two of us for what currently stands as a six-billion-dollar equity portfolio.

On the fixed income side, there's one person who reports to me. She has three people who work for her. She's responsible for both an investment function and a treasury function, because cash flows in and out as we collect premiums or pay claims. So there's a dual aspect to the fixed income role. But yes, we keep the team very lean, without a whole lot of bodies around here.

There are some shops that would hire fifty people to do that 24/7. How much time do you spend analyzing equities and making investment decisions?

I have a joke for a question like that—525,600 minutes which is the theme song from the show *Rent*. That's the number of minutes in a year. I encourage you to listen to that song to hear the whole story.

I have a couple of different hats. The first spectacular thing about my job is that each and every thing I do actually informs and reinforces everything else that I do. So if I were a lawyer keeping a timesheet and trying to bill a client, I do not know how I would split the time, because everything connects.

By the way, our turnover is less than 10 percent a year. We're not trading things in nanoseconds as some large organizations do. We hold things for years, which changes the dynamics a bit. You're sitting here in my office. How often do you hear that phone ring?

It hasn't.

Right. Number two, I'm a director of some other companies. That gives you a fascinating window and insight and perspective about the world of business from somebody else's point of view.

Being inside those board rooms, you can't help but learn and just be informed about business in general, the environment, market conditions, what's good, and what's a challenge, and good people, and not-so-good people. You're getting infinite data points on those kinds of things, all day, every day, when you're in such a setting.

And of course Markel has expanded into ownership and controlling interest in businesses. I'm responsible for the management of businesses, no longer just the ownership of securities. I'm involved in the analysis of potential things that we would buy. Again, that is a fabulous perspective builder where you get to observe and learn things that are going on in the world of commerce. How can you possibly make a decision in isolation? If you are charged with making decisions, it seems like knowing more is better than knowing less. And I'm in this position where I get to learn from a lot of different people and a lot of different settings constantly.

Except for UVA sports, do you have any outside interests or activities that are completely divorced from business and investing?

Not really. Everything connects. To me, joyfully, the way in which our family interacts, the nature of conversations we have around the dinner table, the lessons you learn from playing golf and being frustrated and not having outcomes go the way that you want, are all part of the learning process. As are the value of practice, the limits of practice, and the limits of how much you can actually accomplish. Even hanging around UVA football games or basketball games or going to seminars or reading about history, I'm learning something constantly. No matter where I am or who I'm talking to or what I'm thinking about, there's always something going on that is informing me about life in general. And it all matters.

You're not just the chief investment officer at Markel. You're a co-chief executive officer. Tell me about those expanded responsibilities.

They're different and they're broader. I joke that when you're a CEO, it really means you don't do anything, but you're responsible for everything. I don't know who first said that, but he was exactly right.

When I first came to Markel, Steve gave me a specific task: manage two million dollars. Within a couple of months, he saw how I was doing. He and I would talk about why I was doing this or why I was not doing that. And Steve grew comfortable with my thought process and way of doing things such that he gave me more to look after as time went by.

This is an organization with fourteen thousand people in it, and there are a lot of things going on around here. In no way am I the most competent at doing 13,999 of those tasks that the 14,000 people do. But I am responsible for how it gets done, the spirit of it, the culture of it, the tone of it, and the ultimate financial results.

Harry Truman had a sign on his desk: *The buck stops here*. That's what it's like to be a CEO. You are responsible for everything, and you just do your best to make sure you have the best people operating within the best culture and systems in order to produce the highest odds of a good outcome.

Is it fair to say you spend more time on individual stock selection than trying to predict the macro environment?

Yes. I have zero control over the macro environment. There's really nothing I can do to influence or even predict the macro environment with reasonable enough precision to inform good decisions.

I tend to think about individual companies, individual businesses, and individual people in order to make investment decisions. I'm investing, not trading, so that implies a long-term horizon. That means whatever happens to that business over time is what's going to happen to me as an investor in that business. The price distortion of a good market or bad market gets washed away in the fullness of time. So, is this a company that I'd be happy to own for ten, twenty, thirty years and earn the intrinsic returns of that business? That's really the way I think.

Now that being said, what I just described might apply 80 percent of the time. Ten percent of the time you're going to look around and say I just can't find anything. So you acknowledge that, and maybe have a little bit more liquidity and cash than you normally would. I sense a bit of that in the current environment.

Ten percent of the time, similarly, prices are going to be so attractive across the board that you think, I'm going to invest because there's just no way this can't work out well, over time, if civilization continues to survive. Those kinds of times are obvious, but they are fairly rare.

I might be exaggerating to use an 80/10/10 allocation. It might be 94/3/3. Most of the time, you're operating in the zone of ambiguity. That is the common condition. So any value that I might add by predicting where we are in the continuum is pretty limited, in my experience.

What's been the worst stock pick of your career?

The worst mistake I ever made was not being long stocks; it was being short stocks. From 1984 through 1998 as an accountant, looking at companies and balance sheets, I actually found shorting to be easier than being long. I wasn't sure that something was going to work, but there were some things that I could look at, and I would say with high degrees of confidence, that will never work. I saw things that I thought were a complete piece of BS. So I was naturally pretty good at that.

I consistently made money on the short side every single year I was in business. Every year, until '97/'98, the dot com era. There were certain companies and things that were going on then that I would look at, and I would think, there's no way this is going to work.

What ended up happening is I lost more money shorting in that era than I had made cumulatively in the entire fourteen years before it. I learned painfully what John Maynard Keynes said: "Markets can remain irrational longer than you personally can remain solvent." So somewhere along the line I said *no más*. I stopped. I licked my wounds, and I took what marbles I had left, and said I can't do this anymore. So I stopped being a short seller and have not looked back or done it since.

When you're long stocks, the things that work become bigger and bigger in your portfolio. The things you were wrong about, mathematically, become smaller and smaller in your portfolio.

My grandmother, I would suggest, might have been in the 90th percentile of investors, and here's why. She lived another thirty years or so after my grandfather died in 1964. She was one of those widows that, after my grandfather died, she never made another decision that she didn't have to for the rest of her life. For the next thirty years, she lived in the same house. His suits still hung in the closet. His shoes were on the floor.

And she died owning the same twelve or fifteen stocks that he owned. Among those stocks were Pepsi, Lockheed Martin, and General Public Utilities. She never sold them, and that was a great decision. The other twelve could have gone to zero and it would not have mattered, because those three went up so much that they more than made up for all the mistakes.

Short selling is just the opposite. When you get something right, the most you can make occurs when the stock goes to zero. And that's it. If you're wrong—and I've been wrong so I know this first hand—it can go up and up and up. Your losses are unlimited, versus limited gains. That's bad math. I like the good math of owning things. You can afford to try many things, and you can afford to experiment. You can afford to accept uncertainty and volatility. You'll find, mathematically, some things work and some things don't. But the weighted average return, mathematically, of what you do will be better than the arithmetic average because your right decisions become more important, and your wrong decisions become less important.

I'll tell you a story about traders. At Davenport, Jimmy Thomas was the over-the-counter trader. In 1984 when I joined Davenport, part of the training program consisted of going around and sitting with people who had been with the firm for a while. You'd just spend a day or two or a week with somebody and just observe them, and chat with them, and watch them do their job.

Jimmy Thomas talked about Wards, the predecessor company of Circuit City. That stock would go from six to eight. You bought it at six and sold it at eight. It would go back down to six; you'd buy it, you'd sell it at eight. I thought for a minute and said, "Well you sold it once too often, didn't you?" Circuit City through the '80s or so was the number one stock on the New York Stock Exchange. So he truncated his gain. He made two bucks, and he could've made a thousand. You would have needed to successfully repeat that trade five hundred times. That did not resonate with me in terms of the way I was going to do things.

Now, you do have to pay attention. That's why we go to work every day. You can't completely adopt the pattern that my grandmother did. You do need to be sensitive to a company losing value in a permanent way. There are times you need to sell things and realize some gains. But my strong, strong bias is to try to find things that I can buy and hold on to for a long period of time.

One stock story that worked well was Richfood, here in town. I think it went public at a price of seven or eight bucks, something like that. They were building a new construction project, a huge warehouse. Like many construction projects, it took longer and went over budget. It put the company in a position of financial vulnerability. The stock went down precipitously.

A new man, Don Bennett, came in to run the company. When he was on the job for all of a month, Mike Beall and I from Davenport went to meet him and see what his plan was. Don delivered a preemptory lecture to us about how you run a food distribution business: "Here's how you do it, and here's what I'm going to do." I don't think we asked any question other than how are you, and what is your plan? So we got the lecture delivered to us on the basis of those two very basic questions.

As we walked out, I said to Mike," What do you think?"

"Well I think we just met a forty-eight-year-old guy with fifty-seven years of experience in the grocery business."

He was just this incredibly impressive individual. And everything he said—here's what we need to do, here's why that did not work, here's what we're going to do as a course correction, here's why I think it will work—was an extremely, logical, thoughtful exposition of why they were doing what they were doing. We recommended the stock, and it worked out extraordinarily well.

Here's another investment story that worked out really well. On February 14, 1990, Drexel Burnham declared bankruptcy. Mike Milken, the junk bond king, had been running the firm. The leveraged buyout of

R. J. Reynolds had taken place, the pinnacle deal at that time, *Barbarians at the Gate*.

On that day, every junk bond in the world tanked because Drexel Burnham, the flagship junk bond firm, was going under. Mike Beall and I didn't know anything about junk bonds, but thought, if we were ever going to buy a junk bond, today would be a good day to do it. Which one should we buy?

We talked back and forth, and decided that the most creditworthy company that we knew of, with the best underlying business financed with junk bonds, was RJR. So we looked at RJR bonds, doing some very rough back-of-the-envelope calculations of what the bonds would be worth in liquidation.

RJR had a series of PIK (pay in kind) bonds, no current interest coupon. They were trading at thirty cents on the dollar. Their terms said they had to be reset with current interest payments such that they would trade at par in 1994, three and a half years out. The bonds, trading at thirty cents on the dollar, had to be redeemed, essentially, at one hundred cents on the dollar. By our back-of-the-envelope calculations, we thought they'd be worth seventy cents in a worst case scenario. Well, that seemed like a pretty good risk, so we started buying the bonds.

There were some points you had to know. One, a new tax law required you to accrete the phantom interest income into your current tax year. So you had to pay taxes on the income the bond accrued each year, even though you received no actual cash that year. Most people would not buy the bond, because you have a current tax bill on current income you're not getting, and you have no assurance that the bond will ever pay off. So you could end up paying money to the government while losing money on the bond itself. And the bonds were not really appropriate for IRAs.

This kind of bond was appropriate for almost nobody. But what I happened to know was that Steve and Tony Markel and Alan Kirshner had borrowed money to buy their Markel stock from the second generation of the Markel family. In effect, it was a family leveraged buyout of Markel Corporation prior to the IPO. They could only deduct the interest expense on the loans to buy the stock on their tax returns up to the amount of interest income. So the IRS would not allow the interest expense deduction unless they had offsetting interest income.

Having observed this, I called Steve and said, "Steve, you're the only person in the world who this makes sense for, because you've already got stranded deferred tax assets that are not doing you any good. You can match the bond income against the expense." That was an intriguing notion to Steve, and we bought the bonds on February 14, 1990.

By September of that year, seven months later, the bonds were redeemed at par. That gave Mr. Markel a strong reason to think that Tom Gayner might be a good investment guy.

Do you have another investment story?

When you asked me how I got in the investment business, I can't remember not being in it. As an example, when I was at the University of Virginia, class of '83, think about interest rates at the time. You're talking government bonds at 15 percent and lower-rated bonds even higher.

In those days, you could borrow three thousand dollars on a federal student loan on just your signature. In my memory, you did not accrue any interest while you were in school, and then it was at 3 percent interest rate after that. I borrowed three thousand dollars a year at a 0 percent interest rate and put the money in the T. Rowe Price New Income Fund, which was earning 12, 13, 14 percent a year in interest income. I had built up to twelve thousand dollars in borrowings over four years at zero cost, and then earned 12, 13, 14 percent income on those funds. So the interest arbitrage spread effectively paid a good deal of my tuition by the time I was in my fourth year at UVA. I was always thinking about stuff like that.

I was fourteen years old when IRAs were created. I opened one immediately because of the attraction of tax-deferred compounding over the years. That IRA is still in existence today. I've put money in it almost all the way along. It's a meaningful thing.

The Virginia Prepaid Tuition Plan? When it was created, I had three children—two girls and a boy. Their ages maybe were seven, four, and one. You could prepay tuition and mandatory fees at any Virginia state school. I thought the Commonwealth of Virginia priced the plan extremely attractively from the standpoint of the purchaser, to say it as politely as possible. I borrowed money to buy twelve years of tuition for my three children the first day that the plan was offered.

I like to think I'm a pretty good investor, but I wasn't sure I could keep up with the way tuition prices were rising. Well, after eighteen months or two years, something like that, the Commonwealth figured out that they had mispriced the plans, and stopped selling them. And then new plans came out at much higher prices. But they honored the original ones.

In my analysis, it was like buying a general obligation municipal bond of the Commonwealth of Virginia. You needed to make a judgment about the creditworthiness of Virginia. I felt comfortable with that.

✌

After concluding the interview and turning the recorder off, I asked Tom how he made it through his college graduation day, so soon after his father passed away. Did he attend the ceremonies? Here's a pretty close reconstruction of his answer:

"I didn't walk the Lawn,[42] just couldn't. I asked a teacher friend of mine to pick up my diploma, which he did. It was a sad time for me.

"A couple of years ago, my daughter Mary Gin graduated from UVA. In fact, because she knew what happened at my graduation, she pronounced that I would walk the Lawn with her when she graduated. In the month leading up to her graduation she procured an extra cap and gown for me. She told the story to a group of her friends, and they all surrounded me to get through security.

"During the ceremony, a friend of mine was attending the graduation for his son. He told me later he thought he spotted someone who looked like me among the walking students, 250 feet away, shielded by a crowd of protective young students. He said to his wife, "That looks like Tom Gayner." As I got closer and closer he said, 'That *is* Tom Gayner. What is he doing here?' Later, I told him the whole story of how that came to be."

Was there a dry eye in the house?

"Are you kidding? Sometimes you gotta let it go! That day stands as one of the favorite moments of my life."

XI

THE BIG BOARD

WILLIAM R. JOHNSTON

A graduate of Washington and Lee University, Bill was president of the New York Stock Exchange from 1996 through the end of 2001. Starting as a clerk in 1962, he spent the next thirty-four years on the Exchange floor. He bought a seat in 1964, opened his own specialist firm in 1980, and from 1990 to 1996 was senior managing director of LaBranche & Co., one of the NYSE's oldest and largest specialist firms. The specialist's job (since renamed Designated Market Maker), unique to the New York Stock Exchange, is to ensure fair and orderly markets in allocated stocks, stepping in and buying shares during selling imbalances, and selling shares during buying imbalances. Bill made markets in several Richmond stocks, including Reynolds Metals, Robertshaw Controls, Signet Bank, Circuit City, Best Products, Capital One, and CarMax.

I made my first trade at age fourteen or fifteen, when I borrowed some government bonds from my mother to use as collateral to buy stock. The stock market was breakfast, lunch, and dinner conversation in our home when I was a child. My father had worked for Francis I. duPont in Wilmington, Delaware. He met a man by the name of Harry Lunger, who had the good fortune to be married to a woman named Jane du Pont Lunger, and they created a firm called Johnston & Lunger, a quasi-broker dealer and later a specialist firm on the floor of the New York Stock Exchange.

I worked for my father during the summers. I spent four years at Exeter and four years at Washington and Lee. I was called up to service in 1961 (the Berlin call-up), went to Fort Hood in Killeen, Texas, for a year, and then came back to New Jersey in August of 1962.

I married Betsy Moore, from Wilmington, Delaware, ten days later on August 25, 1962. Betsy, whom I met in Virginia, graduated from Hollins in 1962. She is an important part of my voyage. We are very, very close.

I started in Wall Street shortly after my wedding, the Tuesday after Labor Day 1962. I never worked anywhere else. Forty-one years at the Exchange, either working on the floor or working for the Exchange.

You traded many Richmond stocks in your career. Do you have a story about one of them?

    With initial public offerings, some official or star would buy the first one hundred shares. We'd start with a hundred-share print for that buyer, a marvelous piece of investor relations for a company. You'll have IPOs today open on millions of shares, with the price based on supply and demand. Even then, they'll start with a hundred-share print. When Best Products went public, Jack DeJarnette, a trader at Wheat who attended Washington and Lee, and I bought the first one hundred shares and gifted it to W&L. We did it so Sydney Lewis, the head of Best Products, and Jack and I could say that Washington and Lee was the recipient of the first hundred shares of Best Products stock.[43]

What are some 9/11 recollections?

    I was in a car driven by a Stock Exchange security guard, accompanied by the listing head of our southeast division, on our way to LaGuardia when the first plane struck the North Tower of the World Trade Center. I was going to fly to Richmond to speak before a financial analysts group, and then we were going to pitch a company to switch from Nasdaq to the NYSE. My first thought was, what idiot could fly a small plane into the World Trade Center on a beautifully bright blue, sunny morning? It wasn't until we drove through the East Tunnel that we knew it wasn't a small plane, and that a second plane had struck the South Tower.

    The Exchange occupied three floors—twenty-eight, twenty-nine, and thirty—in the South Tower. A retired cop, a security guard, hustled people out of the South Tower immediately. We lost nobody, and it was entirely due to that security guard. Dick Grasso[44] told him that we wanted to do something for him. The guard said he'd like to ring the bell at the New York Stock Exchange, and he did. I was there with him.

    There are great 9/11 stories from Stock Exchange lore. Dick did something marvelous in the aftermath, arranging for non-corporate types to ring the bell. Firemen, cops, EMTs, anybody other than politicians. When we reopened on September 17, 2001, the Secretary of the Treasury was up there on the balcony. Hillary Clinton was up there, Schumer was up there, Bloomberg was up there, and Giuliani was up there. But Grasso had a cop and a fireman, friends of guys who had given their lives, ring the bell that day. When they walked across the floor you could hear the roar of the cheers from the traders all the way from the Garage out to the Blue Room.[45] It was spectacular. It was emotional.

If you've never seen it, you really want to go to the 9/11 Memorial & Museum at the World Trade Center. There's a silence; there's an awe. There's quietness that just overcomes you. If you don't choke up, I'll be surprised.

Back to the story. When I got out of the car at LaGuardia, a little five-foot-tall Port Authority policewoman yelled that we should get the blankity-blank outta there while we could. They were closing the place down.

So we drove back into New York City, behind a fire engine. We got as far as City Hall, which is about ten blocks north of the Exchange. There were only two directions you could walk: north uptown or east. If you went west, you were in the river; if you went south you were in the bay. So the three of us dumped the car. I walked into a restaurant to buy three bottles of water and three napkins. The guy behind the counter just gave them to us, saying he didn't know if he'd be open the next day. We wetted down the napkins and used them for bandanas around our face.

Grasso made the decision, with the heads of the Treasury and the SEC, to close the Exchange. We didn't open that day or the rest of the week. We held industry meetings, and I was in constant communication with all the brokerage firms, determining their readiness to open, for the next four days. We opened on Monday the seventeenth.

What was another memorable day in your career?

October 19, 1987, with the market down 22.6 percent. I was running a firm, Agora, a market maker in about thirty stocks on the floor of the Exchange. We lost a third of our cash capital on that day. If I had hair, it would have turned white quickly on October 19, 1987.

We closed right on the low on the nineteenth. One of the first things I did once I got off the floor was to go upstairs and call our bank, Irving Trust. I told our banker that I would need to borrow more money than I've ever borrowed in my life. We were going to need somewhere between thirty and thirty-five million dollars. We didn't know exactly what we needed because we were still trying to figure out what our inventories were. I had never borrowed more than ten or twelve million dollars prior to that time. You could hear her gasp over the phone.

Monday night, I made a couple of calls around to other people to find out what they were doing in terms of trying to raise capital. Our good friend, Peter Kellogg, offered capital to firms on Tuesday morning if they needed it to continue to open their stocks and trade their stocks.

I went up to our apartment and got darn little sleep, as you can imagine. I was back downtown by two or three o'clock in the morning and called London. We had a British partner, Smith Brothers (ultimately taken over by the Rothschild family and later by Merrill Lynch). I asked them to try to help us liquidate some stocks. We traded about eight or nine foreign securities at that time, the biggest of which was Glaxo. We were actually able to make some sales in London and raise some capital. European securities tended to trade better in London.

There were buyers on the morning of the twentieth. There had been significant company announcements overnight of stock buybacks. The market opened strong, and many stocks gapped higher: J. P. Morgan, American Express, and other big stocks. Then the market turned around and tanked late morning, early afternoon.

John Phelan, chairman of the Exchange, had told the Fed that his dealers were going to need to borrow lots of money. Phelan had been a specialist himself and knew damn well that specialists were going to need it to pay for stocks they bought. So on Tuesday afternoon the Fed told the New York banks to basically loan the specialist community what they needed to settle those transactions.

Stocks rallied again in the afternoon and closed up dramatically. The story was the Fed had *bought the market*, buying futures and stocks, which was never proven and was probably nothing more than a marvelous rumor.

When is the last time that you walked on the floor of the New York Stock Exchange?

It's close to ten years now. I went back for a tribute to John Phelan.

Do you think there's a future for floor-based trading?

In times of crisis there is always a need for floor-based trading. You need a human to say, hey, let's think about what's going on here.

You know the old fat finger theory, where somebody sends an order in to sell a thousand shares of stock and it became a hundred thousand shares due to a fat finger? We'd see whole baskets of orders where the size was screwed up. You need people that can recognize that kind of thing. You've had too many meltdowns, with stocks going to ridiculous prices, because nobody was there to call a timeout for a chance to think about what was happening.

That type of human judgement was an example of the value of the floor, along with our depth guidelines.[46] Specialists were rated and measured on their effectiveness. We were the market maker in AT&T at LaBranche. *Telephone* went up or down an eighth or maybe a quarter on five or ten thousand shares. It didn't go down a dollar; it didn't go up a dollar. We had to risk our own capital to buy when everyone was selling and sell when everyone was buying, and stocks were taken away from us if we didn't do a good job. That's a value that still exists. The great complaint about Nasdaq was that dealers wouldn't answer their phone in times of crisis. Maybe they would for a very, very good customer, but maybe they wouldn't for a not-so-good customer.

Dick Grasso's philosophy was that if the smallest customer received the right execution, then all customers, small and large, would benefit. If you do what's right for the little guy, you'll probably end up doing what's right for the biggest guy. That was Grasso's credo.

An important belief was that your word is your bond. W&L, with its honor code, probably gave me the first inkling of what it took to say, "Take 'em, sold. I bought 'em, I sold 'em," and never think about welshing on a trade.

In the good old days, if you'd broken the rules, they rang the bell at the Stock Exchange in the middle of the day. If you were floor-based, they read out your sins, and you were escorted off the floor of the Exchange. That's not politically correct anymore, which is a shame. Because when you're a twenty-three-year-old, as I was in 1962, it's one hell of a learning experience. Why would you break the rules for a business that was so good, where we could make the kind of money that we weren't particularly bright enough to deserve? Remember this is back in the days of fixed commissions, when the rates were significantly higher.

Another custom that's disappeared is the grilling of new members on the rules by a committee, followed by the new member signing the constitution of the New York Stock Exchange. They still sign the book, but there's not the kind of training program where you learn the rules and prove that you understand the rules. It's like getting a driver's license without learning how to drive the damn car.

What do Wall Street and Main Street have in common?

What Wall Street did well was raise capital for companies across the United States—and the world, if you will—that needed capital to grow their businesses. Where did those companies go for capital? They went to your local Richmond broker. Richmond had the likes of J. C. Wheat, Scott & Stringfellow, Anderson & Strudwick, and the other brokerage firms headquartered there. And your Richmond broker sold stock to Richmond residents. That is a part of the whole American dream. It's building America through capital formation.

And another piece I'd add is that there were a tremendous number of entrepreneurs in Richmond. Rick Sharp of Circuit City/CarMax, Sydney Lewis of Best Products, Rick Deane of Signet Bank, and others. We were the market maker in Capital One. That was a fascinating story; they created a better way than existing credit card companies of managing risk. There's a hell of a lot of entrepreneurship that came out of Richmond. It's in your DNA. Or maybe it's something in the water.

XII

THE BOND TRADER

A. PLUNKET BEIRNE III

Plunket is with Randolph Square IP, where his asset class specialty has shifted from stocks, bonds, and derivatives to intellectual property with attention to risk management, analytics, and the market applications of patents and innovation. When not looking for the next anecdote, he can often be found coaching field hockey and lacrosse. We met in his Richmond office.

I was managing a restaurant in Charlottesville, Virginia, while still kicking around UVA. One of my best customers, Roger Sager, worked for a firm in Charlottesville: Lee Sager and Company, a New York Stock Exchange execution firm owned by his brother. Roger liked me and offered me a job. That's how I got in the business. Basically, it's because of this guy's habit of drinking lots of Scotch at my bar at night.

I came to Richmond and started at Wheat, First Securities in early November 1990. My wife was trading municipal bonds there at the time, her first job out of college. She introduced me to Shelly Rubin, the branch manager at the Wheat's flagship office in Richmond, who hired me.

I went through the Wheat First new broker/new hire training program even though I'd been in the business for about nine months. Unfortunately, our training class at Wheat First was the last one allowed to go out on the town with product managers after class, which had been a longstanding tradition. Each night a different department would take the training class out for drinks. My training class abused that, so the tradition ended.

You've said that Richmond is different from other financial centers. How so?

Richmond had, at one point, seven New York Stock Exchange members headquartered in town. Charlotte didn't have that. Atlanta didn't have that. I believe the only other town that had as many outside of New York was Chicago. I don't think Los Angeles or San Francisco had seven homegrown New York Stock Exchange member firms. We also had a large bank community because we had a Federal Reserve branch.

We were different from Boston or Philadelphia in other ways. Historically, the financial world (especially in Boston) was centered on asset management, for the same reason Edinburgh was an asset management center. Much of the asset management business grew up around the maritime industry. Captains of ships would leave somebody in charge of their wealth for the benefit of their families when they'd go on a voyage. That is how many asset managers started. The Scottish Widows' Fund is an example.

Those centers weren't like Richmond. In Richmond, if someone thought he could sell a stock or a bond, he could start his own firm. It was very entrepreneurial and very small, but some of the firms grew to be sizeable. One of the bond firms I worked for was Craigie & Company, which was started in 1929 by two brothers. They had thirty dollars of capital and were in business. The financial world in Richmond grew that way. A couple guys with a good idea, who thought they could get somebody to do business with them and thought they knew something about stocks and bonds, could start a financial company. It made Richmond unique. Sometimes you wonder, why not Atlanta? Why didn't Atlanta become a major financial center? I just don't think they had the sort of entrepreneurial environment that Richmond had.

Tell me some of the differences you saw as a trader when you started in the business compared to when you left the business.

When I started at Lee Sager & Company, it was all about stock trading. We would get feedback from the floor of the New York Stock Exchange all day about what's trading, what the trend is, who's seeing what. You would relate that information back to clients. The story would be something like, hey, Lee's standing over at the Dresser Industries booth, and it looks like they're putting together a big book there. It looks to us like the stock's probably good for a half a point gain. That was straight from the floor of the Exchange.

When I first got to Wheat First, with an army of brokers and analysts, we'd get ideas every morning: news about stocks or what stocks might be in play that day. You'd walk into the office and there would be a wall full of research. This stock, that stock, this stock. You could call an analyst. You could get an analyst on the phone and say I have a client with X amount of money. He's asking about this, and he might want to buy a few thousand shares.

It was very much driven by investment ideas. We were in the business to buy low, sell high. In the '90s, right as I was getting into the business, that tide was turning. We were very careful not to be called stockbrokers. We were FAs, financial advisors. It wasn't about having a book of clients who would trade with you anymore. It was about gathering assets. You'd do the math. X amount of assets is going to naturally generate— and I think this is probably still true today—about seventy basis points, or .7 of 1 percent, of commissions to a broker. So if you have a hundred million dollars in assets, you should be a seven-hundred-thousand-dollar producer.

I remember walking by the wall that used to be filled with the analysts' research reports on Philip Morris, Coca-Cola, the furniture industry, and regional banks. I noticed they were disappearing. You'd start to see reports for mutual funds, for annuities, for different products and asset classes. They weren't related to picking stocks.

Management suggested a more *consultative* approach. We were encouraged to look for mutual funds or third-party money managers for clients. You were then on the same side of the table as your client, finding other people whose full-time job was to manage money and pick stocks. You, along with your client, would hire and fire that fund manager.

The training focus moved from how to read a balance sheet and understand stock market signals to how to talk with customers about their tax situation. It became much more of a financial planning job, which is why I left the stock business. I wanted to trade stuff. I wanted to see stuff traded. I wanted to have two phones up to my ears and get deals done, so I went into the bond business.

I had initially gone over to Prudential Securities. I stayed there for eighteen months, and moved to Craigie Inc., in 1995. Craigie was a municipal bond underwriter and traded governments, mortgages, and all sorts of fixed income.

There's a funny story here. Right around the time I was thinking of getting into the business in Charlottesville, I came to Richmond to see what else was available. I interviewed with Allen Ferguson, a senior manager at Craigie, who told me they didn't really have any way to train me. Their people came in with their own accounts and did business right off the bat. There was no one there who could train me, and they didn't have accounts to give me. I had no experience. If I wanted to work at Craigie, I should come back in five or six years and then let's talk.

So, coming back to 1995, I was going through the interview process at Craigie. At the end of the day, I had to meet with the president and the CEO, who was Allen Ferguson. Allen said, why Craigie? Why do you want to come work at the halls of Craigie?

I replied, "Allen, you told me five years ago to go out and get experience and then come back and talk to you. I'm here."

Mr. Ferguson looked at one of the partners and said, "I knew it! I knew it! That's the right guy. That's Craigie material if I've ever seen it." I was offered the job, and I took it. The fact is, I hadn't remembered his comment from five years ago until just that moment. I certainly didn't plan it like that.

BB&T bought Craigie in 1997. I resigned in 2000 and went to work for Advest on Rector Street in New York, where they traded a lot of odd-lot corporate bonds. That was a natural move because, near the end of my time at BB&T, I was already offering Advest's inventory to my clients. I was there for six months, and it was a total disaster.

That job was eye-opening. You go to New York and you think you're going to work for a bunch of grownups. No. It was a total bunch of crazies. The guy who sat next to me would open and close his penknife all day long while making phone calls. *Very* strange. And the guy on the other side of me was named Mongo, for a reason.

The whole floor was just full of crazies. We had one guy who liked to wander around New York City and elbow people on the street. Just throw his shoulder at them. Just liked to see what would happen.

I came back to Richmond as a result of an out-of-the-blue call from John Tracey, who had been sales manager of taxable fixed income at Wheat. I'd known John Tracey, and my wife had worked with him. John was at Ferris, Baker Watts at the time. I told him I was too far along with other interviews, but he was a great salesman. Within three weeks of my telling him no, I started working at Ferris, helping to start a taxable fixed income department. They'd just opened an office in Richmond, which was perfect for me.

I sat on the desk with our mortgage trader. We traded mortgages and agencies in that office, and I also worked with Ballard Parker, who traded both. He had been in the business since the late '60s. Ballard was hired at Ferris to be kind of a consultant, to use his Rolodex to help develop institutional sales. The business grew, and I don't think that Ballard Parker knew that for almost the next ten years he was actually going to make money and be a part of a dynamic taxable fixed income effort.

I was there for eight years, until Royal Bank of Canada bought Ferris in 2008. Some say the sale was partly a response to a broker revolt after my department took a seven-million-dollar write down of CDOs (collateralized debt obligations). We recognized the problem early, before other firms. The financial crash occurred in 2008, but the cracks were clear even in the first quarter of 2007.

We had hired some people in Charlotte to trade CDOs, which were a hot ticket. We did some profitable business. Then, all of a sudden, we owned close to seven million dollars' worth of inventory. And the business dried up. Regular customers weren't buying. Bonds were trading dealer to dealer. It seemed like 1994, when collateralized mortgage obligations (CMOs) became illiquid. All of a sudden CMOs were viewed as toxic waste, and dealers were only trading amongst themselves.

Now it was 2007, and we experienced the same thing with CDOs. We were thinking, we haven't sold a CDO; we haven't traded a CDO to a real account in a while. Why is that? We knew the CDOs were performing, not missing any payments. But if we were to go out on the street and try to sell them, we'd take a huge hit. So our department head decided to keep them, but mark them down in value. That caused a paper loss of around seven million dollars.

Six months or so later, The *Baltimore Sun* got wind of this and called our CEO, Roger Calvert. The *Sun* asked Roger about the write-down. Roger said no comment.

Water was coming through the dike at that point for the entire industry. You heard every day that Merrill Lynch was writing down millions of dollars. The numbers quickly became billions. Bear Stearns was having trouble. Nobody could get a real handle. It wasn't yet June of 2008, but cracks were there.

So I called Roger Calvert, a very accessible CEO, and suggested he call the *Baltimore Sun* back and say the reason we took a seven million dollar hit on these CDOs is because we're geniuses. And then challenge the reporter to call the treasurer of Merrill Lynch and ask him how his day is going. Roger laughed and appreciated the joke, but he never made the call.

It turned out we were right. The last I heard of those CDOs is that they never missed a payment. But if you were a retail broker at Ferris, Baker Watts, a big portion of your retirement was in the company stock. The bond department just took a seven-million-dollar hit. They didn't like that.

I know you have some stories about after-hours socializing with customers.

It used to be that personalities ran the business. You had relationships with someone you could talk to on the phone and go out with and have some fun. Dinner and drinking was a big part of it. And that changed as electronic trading became dominant. The A+ math majors took the business from the C+ history majors. I was very much the C+ history major.

Everybody's favorite client worked at Harris Bank in Chicago. Everybody wanted to go out with him and have fun. You could have drinks with him, and then you'd sell bonds to him. With him, it was a roving fraternity party. He retired, if I remember correctly, in the early '90s.

As the story went—I wasn't there to see it—he and a group of salesmen were out barhopping in Chicago. Early in the evening, they walked by an antiques store, and the customer looked in the window and saw an old whaling harpoon, right out of *Moby Dick*. He said he always wanted one of those. So he went in and bought it. Why not? The store wrapped it in paper. The night was young, and the group was still wandering around Chicago, bar to bar.

Well, the evening ended very late, and some of the guys who were from out of town, including the person from Richmond, had forgotten to make hotel reservations. They ended up spending the night at the customer's house near Lincoln Park, a really nice brownstone.

They got to the house and opened the door. By this point, all the paper was off the harpoon, and the customer was just holding it. He decided he needed to throw it into his front hallway, which is where the harpoon flew before jamming itself into the wall. Everyone went to sleep after that.

The next morning the customer woke up on his sofa, surrounded by his friends. The front door was wide open, with a harpoon sticking out of the wall. Initially, he had no recollection of what had happened. So he called the police, and just as they showed up, his wife came downstairs, shook her head, and explained what happened. Plus a few other comments. He had to explain to the police, "Sorry, that was me."

I had a good client in New York whose name was Henry. Henry was a great guy. The important thing about Henry is Henry had stature. He looked like he was someone important. He grew up in a world where looking important came easy to him. He was a good Harvard man, with famous relatives and important godparents.

One time I was with Henry at the Temple Bar in New York. Walking over to the bar to meet him, some tourists from Pennsylvania stopped me, pointed to Henry, and asked if I knew him. They knew he was important and were trying to figure out who he was.

I don't know why I did this. It certainly wasn't premeditated. But I started explaining to them, in what I felt was a passable Finnish accent, that he was the prime minister of Finland, and I was his personal private secretary. They insisted on meeting him, and I didn't know how Henry would respond. But *he* started speaking to them in a Finnish accent. Henry explained to them that we were in New York on a trade mission and that we wanted to have a Gray's Papaya Hot Dog franchise in Helsinki. They were so excited about this whole thing that they bought us a round of drinks. They were very happy to know that they had met the prime minister. And Henry just went right with it.

One thing I don't think people remember, or perhaps want to remember, is that Peter Madoff, Bernie Madoff's brother, came to Richmond quite often in the '90s. Madoff Securities' legitimate business was trading NYSE listed stocks on the Midwest Exchange. When trading a stock for a customer, after a broker dealer identified the best execution price, the broker would route the order to the cheapest exchange for execution. If the NYSE and the Midwest (Madoff Securities) had the same price, the trade would be sent to Madoff, because it cost twenty dollars and took as long as thirty seconds to complete an order on the NYSE, compared to ten dollars and half the time with Madoff. The Richmond brokerage firms were big Madoff trading customers, and Peter Madoff came to Richmond to visit his clients. I do feel that I need to underline that this had nothing to do with Bernie Madoff's future fraud.

When I started work on Main Street at Wheat, First Securities, you would get out in the morning from your parking place, and the sidewalk was packed with people dressed for work. All the guys were in their suits; all the women were in their dress suits. The shoes that they were going to wear for work were in their bags. Everybody was going to restaurants getting a breakfast sandwich. The sidewalk was busy, everybody moving around. Things change. I recall standing on the same corner one morning in 2003 with Ballard Parker. The traffic light actually clicked twice before a car went through.

I came in at the end of an era in the financial services industry, and am very grateful that I was able to meet and work with some tremendous characters for which the community is legend. There are hundreds of stories and anecdotes about the people, the clients and the professionals, and the adventures of doing business. I'm sure that the seemingly sterile and faceless processes of modern electronic investing will have its own stories, but they won't have quite the same Homeric proportions as yesterday, when a large collection of overly gregarious people tried to develop multiple, disparate relationships, all to get good business done. ∎

XIII

AFTER THE BELL

HORACE EDWARD MANN

Chip was born in Petersburg and has held a variety of governmental and political positions, including directing the activities of thirty-seven federal agencies and innumerable state, local, and foreign groups while serving as executive director of the Jamestown 400th Commemoration Commission. He's also author of a terrific book, The Queen and the USA, *which documents the three state visits to Virginia made by Queen Elizabeth II of the United Kingdom. Soon after graduating from the College of William & Mary (where his son also graduated), Chip was appointed to its Board of Visitors, the youngest appointee ever. We caught up at the Continental Lounge, where he offered up some recollections of one of his early "political" jobs . . . a waiter at W. T. O'Malley's.*

Jerry Waters, the first proprietor and developer of O'Malley's, was the fundraising director for the John Dalton gubernatorial campaign in 1977. (I was John Dalton's driver the last four months of the campaign.) After that campaign, I worked for Linwood Holton, who sought, but lost, the nomination for the Senate seat that eventually John Warner won. Jerry called me afterward and said I know you're in between campaigns right now and things might be a little tough. I'm opening a restaurant. Why don't you come down and help me finish?

So I went in and varnished and vacuumed and cleaned and painted, and was in the first crew that opened O'Malley's, in July of 1978. My first customer was the attorney general of Virginia, Marshall Coleman, and his wife.

Jerry had brought in a very diverse group of investors to help support the restaurant, including Jeff MacNelly, the editorial cartoonist, and Bill Royall, press secretary for the governor. O'Malley's became *the* political bar in Richmond and was high up there in the financial community, also. It was mostly politics, but then the finance crowd discovered it. A lot of bigwigs, including CEOs and lawyers, came in. It was one of those places where a lot of really talented and well-placed people hung out.

I was twenty-three in 1978. One of the fringe benefits of O'Malley's was that many women who worked at The Tobacco Company would come by in the afternoon and have lunch before going to work. So if you slipped them an extra beer, you'd go down to The Tobacco Company after you got off work and they'd slip *you* an extra beer. The more important thing, though, is I was hanging out with all these good-looking women.

There weren't that many restaurants on Main Street, not like now. There were the old fuddy-duddy places, like the Captain's Grill, that were kind of nice but expensive. Shockoe Slip was just taking off. Gatsby's, The Warehouse, Sam Miller's and The Tobacco Company were the first four.

How did Jerry pick the name W. T. O'Malley's?

We had some fun as to what the W. T. stood for. It was just a name picked out of the blue. Jeff MacNelly painted a portrait of a Mr. W. T. O'Malley, a guy with a bartender's apron and a walrus mustache, in his mid-fifties, kind of glaring at you. And that was W. T. O'Malley.

Also, as an ode to Virginia, there was the wonderful painting of Secretariat, in mid-stride, on the wall across the bar. Joe Court, who worked there, painted it. Many of the bartenders and wait staff were pretty accomplished (except me!). There were law students and a playwright. The staff was interesting, and Jerry was interesting, and he drew an interesting crowd, and we had a good time.

Jerry owned O'Malley's from '78 to around '84. The new owners kept the ambiance of the place. They auctioned off all the furniture and equipment and items when they sold it in 1989. My wife and I drove down from Washington to buy a couple of things. If there was an article about an employee in the newspaper, Jerry would frame it and hang it up. There were a few framed articles about me that I wanted to buy, but by the time we arrived, people had already bought them.

O'Malley's had some interesting pictures. One was a signed picture of Nelson Rockefeller, whom Jerry had worked for, giving somebody the finger. Another was an autographed picture of Paul Trible. Jeff MacNelly, being an editorial cartoonist, had a lot of stock pictures of many politicians. One was of U Thant, the former Secretary-General of the United Nations, from Burma. U Thant died, so Jeff didn't need the picture anymore. Jeff signed it, "To Jerry with love, U," and framed it and put it up on the wall.

What was O'Malley's before it was O'Malley's?

I think it was an office supply store, in an old brownstone. Now it's a parking deck.

What was your next job after O'Malley's?

I did some research for the Republican Party of Virginia and then was hired to work in the Secretary of the Commonwealth's office.

Do you have any good backroom political stories that we haven't heard?

In August 1978, when we'd been open just a month, Dick Obenshain, who won the Republican nomination for U.S. Senate over Linwood Holton and John Warner, was killed in an airplane crash. The funeral was on a Saturday. Several of we employees were asked to be ushers. I knew Dick very well. I'd worked against him, but he and I had a great relationship.

The question for the Republican Party was: Now what do we do? What is the process for selecting a new nominee, and who's that going to be? On the Friday night before the funeral, the Holtons came into the restaurant for dinner. It was the Governor and Mrs. Holton and one or two of the kids. About fifteen minutes later, Governor John Dalton and Mrs. Dalton arrived, in a big limo. Mrs. Dalton sat with Mrs. Holton at a table, and we didn't let anybody else in. We cleared out the back of the restaurant and Governor Holton and Governor Dalton sat in the back and talked.

I kept everybody out of the back and waited on them. They must have talked for twenty minutes, thirty minutes. Just the two of them. Then everybody left.

The next day, Governor Holton had those of us who had worked for him meet him in a suite with his family in the Hotel John Marshall to discuss the next step. Should he contend for the nomination? Should he back out? Should he throw an endorsement behind somebody? There weren't enough chairs in his suite, so I sat on the floor, and we talked about whether he should run again. There were about fifteen of us in the room, and everybody got to voice an opinion, including his family.

His daughter Tayloe said she didn't want him to run, because the nominating process had been so brutal when he lost earlier. Holton said, "OK, that's it, move on." He turned to the person next to her, who said, "Well I think you ought to run and here's why." The next person said, "I think you ought to endorse somebody and here's why." Then it was my turn, and I said, "You all don't understand. You all didn't pick up on what he said to his daughter. He's decided not to do it." And he looked at me and smiled and said, "You're the only one that got it." He had decided not to run.

Now what has that got to do with O'Malley's? I think that if John Dalton said in the backroom the night before, "I'll endorse you. I'll work for you. We'll make it happen," Governor Holton would have been all in. But he didn't hear that. He heard, "Well here are the pluses. Here are the minuses. I think you've got an uphill road. You do what you want to do." And I think Linwood thought, I don't need this. I'm not going to run.

I think what John Dalton said was that he couldn't be in a position of sticking his neck out. Which is what he would've done, and I can't blame him. At that time, Dalton was the leader of the Republican Party, which had just suffered a huge loss. And as it turned out, John Warner barely won against Andy Miller.

I'm apparently the last person, except for Linwood Holton, to know about that conversation. And it happened in O'Malley's.

Warner got the nomination the following weekend, at a state central committee meeting. He and Elizabeth Taylor came in O'Malley's a couple of times during the next four or five months. We put them in the back so they'd be obscured from the front windows.

Was there a Democratic counterpart to O'Malley's?

No, but there didn't need to be, because we had a lot of Democrats come in. Chuck Robb's picture was on the wall. Walter Emroch used to come in. I think Andy Miller came in. Henry Howell? He never came in. ∎

Ron, along with four junior high classmates in Northside Richmond, formed The Centaurs, a rock band that has entertained crowds in the Richmond area since 1964. Their breakthrough 1969 recording, "If I Didn't Have a Dime," remains one of the most popular beach music records ever. Ron Moody and The Centaurs were inducted into the Carolina Beach Music Association Hall of Fame in 2008. They're still going strong.

Tom Maeder, a well-known stockbroker at A. G. Edwards and Wells Fargo for years, was important in the band's early success. He was a great friend, a real character, a natty dresser, and a man with a very sharp wit. Before working on Main Street, Tom was a booking agent and handled many of our early gigs. One of my most cherished memories was opening for The Showmen at Tantilla for the very first time. The place was packed, and I still have that framed poster on my office wall. Tom booked us on that show and many after, with some of the most well-known entertainers of the day.

You've been recording for a long time. Where did it start?

Saturday, December 26, 1964, at Lakeside Community Center. If you recall, this was the height of the British Invasion. We passed the hat and made fourteen dollars.

And the rest is history. You recorded hits and signed a deal with Columbia Records when you were still a kid.

We signed our first recording contract with Columbia in 1969. They signed us after our recording of "If I Didn't Have A Dime." We traveled to Baltimore in the spring of '69 to record it and when we returned home, we released it on a local label. From there, it made its way to WLEE, Richmond's powerhouse pop station back in the day. The program director loved the song and played it over the phone for one of his contacts at CBS in New York. He, too, liked the song and within a matter of weeks, we were signed, and it was subsequently re-issued on the famous Columbia red label.

In later years, we also signed deals with MGM and ABC/Dunhill Records. By the early 1980s, I was a music rep during the week, a band leader/singer/entertainer on the weekends, and, for a time, owner of a recording studio.

You must have played in every venue in the region, for all types of audiences.

It's probably easier for me to name the places we *haven't* performed. Certainly, many folks will remember Tantilla, The Wigwam, and Tilly's, just to mention a few names. We've had gigs at every hotel ballroom downtown, such as the Marriott, Jefferson, Omni, John Marshall, and so on. We played at one private fortieth birthday party downtown for a stockbroker (I think), on a date that happened to be my fortieth birthday, as well. I joined the revelry, and a good time was indeed had by all.

Today I've retired from the record labels, but I'm still playing lots of music, writing, publishing, hosting two radio shows, and co-hosting a monthly lecture series on the history of rock and roll.

As a Richmond resident most of my life, I've noticed the ebbs and flows and changes in Richmond's downtown area. For a while there wasn't much building activity. The Jefferson was essentially closed. Then a few of the bigger buildings like the Bank of America building on Main Street, the Federal Reserve Bank on Byrd Street, and the SunTrust building on Main, were built in the 1970s and 1980s. Of course, the beautiful Central Fidelity Bank building had been on Broad Street forever. New hotels opened. Younger people started coming downtown again, and we played many gigs there as a result.

If you lived in Richmond, you recognized the local broker names like Wheat, Scott & Stringfellow, and Branch, Cabell. I guess most of them have merged with bigger companies now. My observation on stockbrokers who work on Main Street? They can certainly party with the best of 'em!

XIV

ANNE HOBSON FREEMAN
AND CARLYLE TILLER

F. CARLYLE TILLER

As a newly minted Wharton School MBA in 1950, Carlyle Tiller considered working for Merrill Lynch in New York City. Instead, a twenty-nine-year-old Jim Wheat, Jr. persuaded him to join the tiny firm of J. C. Wheat & Company in his hometown of Richmond. A close confidant to Mr. Wheat for the next thirty-six years, Carlyle Tiller was a director of research, general partner, and, from 1971 until his retirement in 1986, chief executive officer of what became Wheat, First Securities. Mr. Tiller graduated from the University of Richmond and later served as rector of the school's board of trustees. He died in 2015.

As part of her research that resulted in A Hand Well Played: The Life of Jim Wheat, Jr., *published in 1994, Mrs. Anne Hobson Freeman interviewed dozens of individuals who knew Jim Wheat, including his family, friends, and Main Street executives. Carlyle Tiller's interview was conducted September 5, 1991, eight months before Mr. Wheat died in his office at Riverfront Plaza. It's a rare and personal insight into the legendary Richmond financier. The Virginia Historical Society allowed me to include a portion of the Tiller interview, which follows.*

AHF questions are in italics.

Explain to me what Jim Wheat did.

He was the deal man. Jim and I were partners, but he was the senior partner. There was no question about that in my mind. He was such a unique human being. I would pass points by Jim to get his input, which was always worth its weight in gold. Then it was up to me to implement the plan. I didn't do administrative things alone, because he was right there with me all the time, giving me input, but he didn't spend his time putting the plans into effect. It would have been a waste of his time to do that.

He was Mr. Outside; I was Mr. Inside. He was involved in so many things. His contacts were unbelievable, and he had the ability to get business, big business. One of our big events was becoming a lead underwriter for VEPCO. Back in the late 1970s, when VEPCO needed money for expansion, we were one of three bankers – Merrill Lynch, Morgan Stanley, and Wheat. That couldn't have happened without Jim Wheat. That's just one example. It was due to Jim's ability to meet people on their own terms and to think the business issues through. On the other hand, we had to have an organization that could carry things out. That was my job, to see if we could carry out what Jim Wheat developed.

If you were writing a sketch of Jim, what would you stress, his creativity?

Gosh, there are so many things. Of course, his mental strengths are just uncanny: his ability to concentrate, his ability to think logically, his ability to remember. That's due to his blindness. He goes into a room, he's got to remember where every piece of furniture is. When he goes to a dinner party or cocktail party, it's not an accident that he doesn't knock things over. It's all mental. He just has a mind that is not comparable to an average person's mind.

I've always said that if you pick anybody in the country, and I have Jim Wheat, and there's a complex, difficult business problem, Jim Wheat will get to the answer first. I've seen it. I've seen him negotiate with the top bankers in the country and he could always add up. Always.

There are other things that people may not notice as much, like his compassion. He's a tough businessperson and doesn't give an inch in negotiations. He could think so much faster than other people and he could articulate so well that he could usually get his way. But on the other hand, he's just as soft on people's problems, people that are in trouble.

Jim never bent on integrity. In fact, integrity was the most important factor in working with people.

The second is loyalty. And then brain-power third?

That's the way he wanted it. I used to think, "Well, the brain is everything." But I learned that he was right. Integrity, Number One; loyalty, Number Two; and brain-power, Number Three. He had all those things in equal parts.

Jim had visions, but not pie-in-the-sky visions. They were visions that could be carried out. And Jim was a doer, despite the fact that he was very bright.

He is action oriented.

He had a sense of urgency about him. He didn't talk about a problem and say, "Well, we'll do that tomorrow." He would do it now! [Snaps his fingers] Get on the phone, pick up the phone!

The word that is probably used the most in describing Jim is "inspirational." To me, the word would be "force." Jim Wheat is a force, not just an inspiration. He's a mental force. He's a moral force. You feel it, the strength, the intensity of the man. You can't deny it. ■

Source: Anne Hobson Freeman papers,
Virginia Historical Society; interview with
Carlyle Tiller, September 5, 1991.
Courtesy of Anne Hobson Freeman

APPENDICES, NOTES, AND CREDITS

.

Appendix A

SELECTED STOCK BROKERAGE FIRMS IN RICHMOND: 1960–2000

1960

Abbott Proctor & Paine	911 East Main Street; 4110 Fitzhugh Avenue
Anderson & Strudwick	807 East Main Street
Branch, Cabell & Co.	814 East Main Street
Branch & Co.	1015 East Main Street
F. W. Craigie & Co.	616 East Main Street
Davenport & Co.	1113 East Main Street
R. S. Dickson & Co.	Travelers Building
Francis I. duPont	729 East Main Street
Galleher & Co.	Mutual Building
Merritt King & Co.	920 East Main Street
Scott & Stringfellow	Mutual Building
J. C. Wheat & Co.	1001 East Main Street
Willis Kenney & Ayres Inc.	205 West Franklin Street

1970

Anderson & Strudwick	913 East Main Street
Branch, Cabell & Co.	814 East Main Street
Branch & Co.	1015 East Main Street
Cecil-Waller Company	906 No. Thompson Street
Craigie Inc.	616 East Main Street
Davenport & Co.	801 East Main Street
F. I. duPont, Glore, Forgan & Co.	629 East Main Street
Galleher & Co.	Mutual Building
Martin W. Harowitz & Co.	1904 Byrd Avenue
Clarence H. Holding & Co.	1001 East Main Street
Lane Sterling & Co.	1004 No. Thompson Street
Legg Mason & Co.	5017 West Broad Street
Mason-Hagan Investments	Fidelity Bankers Building

Mason & Lee Inc.	1001 East Main Street
Merrill Lynch Pierce Fenner & Smith	700 East Main Street
Miller & Patterson	Mutual Building
Paine Webber Jackson & Curtis	830 East Main Street
Scott & Stringfellow	Mutual Building
Thomson & McKinnon Auchincloss	Ross Building
Wheat & Co. Inc.	801 East Main Street

1980

Alex. Brown & Sons	1 James River Plaza
Anderson & Strudwick Inc.	1108 East Main Street
Branch, Cabell & Co.	1015 East Main Street
Cecil Waller & Sterling Inc.	906 No. Thompson Street
Craigie Inc.	9th & Main Streets
Daley & Co.	1 No. 5th Street
Davenport & Co. of Virginia	801 East Main Street
Dean Witter Reynolds	700 East Main Street
Exchange Services Inc.	108 So. Leadbetter Rd.
Ferris & Co.	2707 East Grace Street
Galleher & Co.	Mutual Building
Martin W. Harowitz & Co.	1500 Forest Avenue
Heritage Investments Inc.	6606 West Broad Street
Kingsley Boyd & Southwood Inc.	Richmond
Merrill Lynch Pierce Fenner & Smith	F&M Center, 12th & Main Streets
Paine Webber Jackson & Curtis Inc.	830 East Main Street
Scott & Stringfellow Inc.	Mutual Building
Thomson McKinnon Securities Inc.	6620 West Broad Street
Wheat First Securities Inc.	707 East Main Street

1990

A. G. Edwards	7204 Glen Forest Drive
Advest Inc. —	
Cecil Waller & Sterling Div.	6800 Paragon Place
Alex. Brown & Sons	100 Shockoe Slip
Anderson & Strudwick Inc.	1108 East Main Street
Branch, Cabell & Co.	919 East Main Street

Broker's Exchange Inc.	530 East Main Street
Coleman Edwards Securities Corp.	1901 East Franklin Street
Craigie Inc.	823 East Main Street
Crestar Securities Corp.	919 East Main Street
Davenport & Co. of Virginia	801 East Main Street
Dean Witter Reynolds	600 East Main Street
Edward D. Jones	Ashland
Exchange Services	Ashland
Financial Corp. of Virginia	1313 East Main Street
First Wachovia Brokerage Services	9100 Arboretum Parkway
Martin W. Harowitz & Co.	1500 Forest Avenue
Merrill Lynch Pierce Fenner & Smith	Sovran Center Pavilion, 12th & Main Streets
Olde Discount	Richmond
Paine Webber	1021 East Cary Street
Private Ledger Financial Services	804 Moorefield Park Drive
Prudential Bache Securities	900 East Main Street
Quick & Reilly Inc.	101 Shockoe Slip
Richmond Financial Corp.	1001 East Main Street
Scott & Stringfellow Inc.	909 East Main Street; 901 Moorefield Park Drive
Securities Research Inc.	1001 East Main Street
Shearson Lehman Hutton	629 East Main Street
Sovran Investment Corp.	12th & Main Streets
Wheat First Securities Inc.	707 East Main Street

2000

A. G. Edwards	1313 East Main Street
Advest	6800 Paragon Place
Anderson & Strudwick Inc.	707 East Main Street
J. C. Bradford & Co.	951 East Byrd Street
Branch, Cabell & Co.	919 East Main Street
Charles Schwab & Co.	700 East Main Street
Craigie Incorporated	823 East Main Street
Davenport & Company LLC	901 East Cary Street
Deutsche Banc Alex Brown	100 Shockoe Slip
Edward Jones	Eight area offices

Ferris, Baker Watts	901 East Cary Street;
	629 East Main Street
First Union Securities	901 East Byrd Street
Martin W. Harowitz	1201 Dinwiddie Avenue
IJL Wachovia	951 East Byrd Street
Legg Mason Wood Walker	951 East Byrd Street
Merrill Lynch Pierce Fenner & Smith	707 East Main Street
Morgan Keegan & Co.	951 East Byrd Street
Morgan Stanley Dean Witter	600 East Main Street
Northeast Securities	8014 Midlothian Turnpike
Olde Discount Stockbrokers	11440 Midlothian Turnpike
PaineWebber	1021 East Cary Street;
	6620 West Broad Street
Prudential Securities Inc.	1051 East Cary Street
Quick & Reilly Inc.	104 Shockoe Slip
Robert Thomas Securities	West Point
Salomon Smith Barney Inc.	1051 East Cary Street
Scott & Stringfellow Inc.	909 East Main Street;
	808 Moorefield Park Drive
Scottsdale Securities	7110 Forest Avenue
Securities Research Inc.	5413 Patterson Avenue
Spear Leeds & Kellogg	4701 Cox Road
TD Waterhouse Investors Services	701 East Franklin Street

Source: Yellow Pages

Appendix B

SELECTED REGIONAL STOCK AND BOND QUOTES
AT YEAR-END — 1979, 1989, 1999

Year-End 1979*	Bid	Asked
VIRGINIA OVER-THE-COUNTER		
Chesapeake Bay Bridge and Tunnel (Series C bond) 5¾	65	69
BANKS AND INSURANCE		
Central Fidelity	12 ½	13 ¼
Col. Am. Bankshrs	9 ¼	10
Dom. Bankshrs	15 ½	16 ¼
F&M National	11 ½	13
First Col. Life	29 ½	31 ½
First & Merchants	20 ¼	21
Home Beneficial	19 ¾	20 ¾
Jefferson Bnkshrs	13 ½	15 ½
United Va. Bnkshrs	25 ⅛	25 ⅜
Virginia Natl Bnkshrs	13 ⅝	14 ⅛
MISCELLANEOUS		
Alleg Bev	3 ⅞	4 ⅛
Am. Filtrona	12 ⅞	13 ⅜
Basset Furn	17 ½	18 ¼
Brenco	19 ¼	20 ¼
Clftn Fg – Wsbo Tel	29 ½	31
Crad-Terry Shoe	10 ½	11
Dibrell Bros	12 ¾	13 ¾
Doughtie Foods	2 ¾	3 ¾
Heilig Myers	9 ½	10 ½
Heritage Finl	4 ¾	5 ¾
Hop In Foods	13	15
James Riv Corp	18 ¼	19 ¼
Lane Co.	24	25
Old Dom REIT	6 ⅜	6 ⅞
Owens Min Bod	12 ½	13 ½

	Bid	Asked
Pulaski Furn	9 ¾	10 ½
RF&P	210	
Royster	13 ⅜	13 ¾
Smithfield Fds	7 ⅜	8
Stewart Sandwch	3 ⅛	3 ⅝
Tultex Corp	8	9

* Quotes as of January 4, 1980

Year-End 1989**	*Bid*	*Asked*
VIRGINIA OVER-THE-COUNTER		
Chesapeake Bay Bridge and Tunnel (Series C bond) 5 ¾	92	94
FINANCIAL ISSUES		
BB&T Financial	20	20 ¼
Central Fidelity	32	32 ¼
Crestar Fin Corp	28 ⅞	29 ⅛
Dominion Bnkshrs	19 ½	19 ¾
F&M National Corp	13 ¾	14 ¼
Fidelity federal	8 ½	9 ½
Hanover Bank	9 ½	10 ½
Heritage Finl	⅜	½
Home Beneficial	36 ½	37
Investors Finl	4 ½	4 ¾
Jefferson Bnkshrs	23 ½	24 ½
Markel Corp	22	22 ¾
Pioneer Finl	9 ⅞	10 ⅛
Scott & Stringfellow	8 ½	9 ½
United Dominion Rlty	17 ⅞	18 ⅛
Va Beach Fed Savings	4 ⅜	4 ⅝
MISCELLANEOUS		
American Filtrona	26 ¼	28
American Woodmark	6 ⅞	7 ⅛
Bassett Furniture	36 ½	37
Brenco Inc	7 ½	7 ¾
Cadmus Communic Corp	9	9 ¾
CFW Comm Corp	38	

Consumat Systems	2 ⅝	3 ⅛
Dibrell Brothers	23 ¼	24
Doughties Foods	5 ⅞	6 ⅜
DSC Communications	15 ⅜	15 ½
Figgie Intl Holdings A	64	66 ½
Hechinger Co. A	12 ½	12 ¾
Hilb Rogal & Hamilton	18	18 ½
MCI Comm Corp	40 ¼	40 ⅜
Pulaski Furniture	19	19 ½
RF&P	27 ¾	28 ½
Richfood Holdings A	4 ¾	5
S&K Famous Brands	12 ¼	12 ¾
Smithfield Foods	12	12 ½
Stewart Sandwiches	1 ½	1 ¾
WLR Foods	24 ¼	24 ¾

*** Quotes as of January 5, 1990*

Year-End 1999***   *Close*

REGIONAL STOCKS

AMF Bowling Inc.	3 ⅛
Albemarle Corp.	19 ³⁄₁₆
America Online	75 ⅞
Am Woodmark	24 ¼
BB&T Corp.	27 ⅜
Basset Furn	16
Bell Atlantic	61 ⁹⁄₁₆
CFW Communications	34 ¾
CSX Corp	31 ⅜
Cadmus Comm	8 ½
Capital One Fincl	48 ³⁄₁₆
Chesapeake	30 ½
Circuit City Stores	45 ¹⁄₁₆
Circ City CarMax	2 ⁵⁄₁₆
Dan River Inc	5 ⅛
Dominion Res	39 ¼
Eskimo Pie	7 ⅜

Ethyl Corp	3 ½
F&M National Corp	27 ⁹⁄₁₆
Fst Va Banks	43
Freddie Mac	47 ¹⁄₁₆
Gen Electric	154 ¾
Heilig-Meyers	2 ¾
Hilb Rogal Ham	28 ¼
Kmart	10 ¹⁄₁₆
LandAmerica Fin Group	18 ⅜
Markel Corp	155
Media General	52
Newport News Ship	27 ½
Owens & Minor Inc	8 ¹⁵⁄₁₆
Philip Morris	23
Pittston Brink's	22
Pulaski Furniture	15 ½
RJ Reynolds Tobacco	17 ⅝
Reynolds Metals	76 ⅝
S&K Famous Brands Inc	5 ⁵⁄₁₆
Sears Roebuck	30 ⅜
7-11 Inc	1 ²⁵⁄₃₂
Smithfield Foods	24
Smurfit-Stone Cont	24 ½
Stanley Furn	18 ⅜
SunTrust Banks	68 ¹³⁄₁₆
Tredegar Corp	20 ¹¹⁄₁₆
Utd Dominion Realty	9 ⅞
Universal Corp	22 ¹³⁄₁₆
WLR Foods	5 ¾
Wachovia Corp	68
Westvaco	32 ⅝

*** *Quotes as of December 31, 1999*

Source: *Richmond Times-Dispatch*

Appendix C

SELECTED RICHMOND MERGERS AND ACQUISITIONS

Buyer	Seller	Date	Value $ Millions
Carter Hawley Hale Stores, Inc.	Thalhimer Brothers, Inc.	1978	71
First & Merchants Corp.	Virginia National Bankshares, Inc.	1983	NA
Kevin Donohoe and management	Miller & Rhoads (Campeau Corp.)	1987	65
Union Pacific Corp.	Overnite Transportation Co.	1987	1,200
American Home Products	A. H. Robins Co.	1988	700
Adler & Shaykin	Best Products Co.	1988	1,100
Citizens & Southern Corp.	Sovran Financial Corp.	1990	NA
CSX Transportation and VRS	RF&P and public shareholders	1991	350
BB&T Corp.	Craigie Inc.	1997	23
First Union Corp.	Signet Banking Corp.	1997	3,300
Wachovia Corp.	Central Fidelity Banks Inc.	1998	2,300
First Union Corp.	Wheat First Butcher Singer	1998	471
SunTrust Banks, Inc.	Crestar Financial Corp.	1998	9,500

Buyer	Seller	Date	Value
			$ Millions
BB&T Corp.	Scott & Stringfellow Financial Inc.	1999	131
Supervalue Inc.	Richfood Holdings Inc.	1999	1,500
Alcoa Inc.	Reynolds Metals Co.	2000	4,500
Tucker Anthony Sutro	Branch, Cabell & Co. Inc.	2000	21
Georgia Pacific Corp.	Fort James Corp. (James River)	2000	11,000
CoolBrands International Inc.	Eskimo Pie Corp.	2000	35
Cenveo Inc.	Cadmus Communications Corp.	2007	30
Willis Group Holdings	Hilb, Rogal & Hobbs Co.	2008	2,100
Sterne Agee Group	Anderson & Strudwick, Inc.	2011	NA

Sources: Company records; Virginia Historical Society;
"Gone but Not Forgotten," Richmond.com, June 26, 2016;
"Style and Service," October 6, 2012; Roanoke.com

Appendix D

SELECTED RICHMOND BANKRUPTCIES

Company	Date
Freedlander Inc., The Mortgage People	1988
Fidelity Bankers Life Insurance Co.	1991
Best Products, Inc.	1991 and 1996
Investors Savings Bank	1991
Heilig-Meyers Co.	2000
LandAmerica Financial Group	2008
Circuit City Corp.	2008
Chesapeake Corp.	2008
S&K Famous Brands Inc.	2009

Sources: "Gone But Not Forgotten," Richmond.com,
June 26, 2016; "Former Richmond Banker
Eric Freedlander Arrested, Charged in Fraud Case,"
The Washington Post, February 14, 1991.

NOTES

1. "Jefferson Smurfit in Recycling Deal," *New York Times,* March 30, 1990.
2. The Miller & Rhoads and Thalhimers department store names disappeared in 1990. "Gone but Not Forgotten," Richmond.com, June 26, 2016.
3. Jerry W. Markham, *A Financial History of the United States* (New York: M. E. Sharpe, 2002).
4. "The Merrill Lynch Story," an unpublished presentation given by Donald T. Regan to The Newcomen Society, December 4, 1980. Courtesy of George T. Baskerville.
5. Branch Papers, Virginia Historical Society; Richmond Public Library; Patteson Branch, Jr., and Carlisle Branch.
6. David D. Ryan, *Harvest of a Quiet Eye – A Portfolio of East Main Street, Richmond, Virginia* (Richmond: Doryann Press, 1969).
7. Mr. Kellogg's medallion gift had the seal of the New York Stock Exchange on one side, and an inscription noting the dates (1952–1958) that Mr. Scott served on the Exchange's board of governors on the reverse side.
8. J. Harvie Wilkinson, Jr., former chairman of United Virginia Bankshares. His career with UVB and its predecessors spanned 1929–1971.
9. Citizens & Southern National Bank.
10. John Bruce, John Flippin, and Greg Porter.
11. "Pink Sheets" describes a daily publication with quotes for thousands of small stocks ineligible for listing elsewhere. The quotes were printed on pink paper.
12. Richmond, Fredericksburg, and Potomac Railroad.
13. Dell bought EMC for $67 billion in 2015.
14. Oracle bought Micros for $5 billion in 2014.
15. Lucent Technologies bought Ascend for $24 billion in 1999.
16. Pilgrim's Pride bought WLR Foods for $240 million in 2000.
17. Head trader at Davenport.
18. Head trader at Wheat.
19. Small Order Execution System.
20. At various times branch manager, COO, CEO, and chairman of the board at Branch, Cabell & Co.
21. Royal Bank of Canada.
22. CreditTrust was a stock recommended by this editor.
23. GEICO's chief investment officer.
24. "Warren Buffett's Six Best Investments of All Time," *Fortune*, October 31, 2014.
25. "The Trader," *Barron's*, September 21, 1987.

26. "S&P 500 Could Hit 4,300 Within Nine Years," *Barron's*, May 30, 2015.

27. Designated Order Turnaround.

28. Chairman and chief executive officer of Ferris, Baker Watts & Co.

29. Regan, "The Merrill Lynch Story."

30. "Merrill Lynch, Expanding in City, Had an Ancestor Here, History Says," *Richmond Times-Dispatch*, December 26, 1991. Gwathmey & Co., a Richmond cotton trading firm dating to 1820, merged with stockbroker E. A. Pierce in 1926, which merged with Merrill Lynch in 1939.

31. As of June 2017.

32. California Public Employees' Retirement System and California State Teachers' Retirement System, respectively.

33. Treasury Inflation Protected Securities.

34. BlackRock, Inc. is a New York-based global investment management corporation with over six trillion dollars in assets.

35. Kenneth Feinberg, appointed by President Obama as Special Master for TARP Executive Compensation ("pay czar").

36. Lehman Bros. filed for bankruptcy September 15, 2008.

37. Rick Wagoner, GM chief executive officer and Richmond native.

38. Frederick Henderson, former GM chief operating officer, replaced Rick Wagoner as chief executive officer.

39. President of Virginia Commonwealth University and the VCU Health System.

40. *The New York Times*, August 31, 2009, citing a report by the Milliman consulting firm.

41. Vice Chairman at Markel Corporation.

42. The awarding of degrees, and focal point of Final Exercises.

43. It was not the last Best Products stock given to the school; Sydney and Frances Lewis donated Best Products stock valued at nine million dollars to the W&L Law School in the early 1970s.

44. Chairman and chief executive officer of the NYSE from 1995 to 2003.

45. The *Garage* and the *Blue Room* were additional trading areas next to the NYSE's main floor.

46. Depth guidelines require market makers to provide liquidity and curb intraday volatility in NYSE listed securities.

PHOTO CREDITS

Front Cover—"The Corner," Painting by William P. Schubmehl. Reproduced with permission of the artist and Scott & Stringfellow.

Muldowney: *Traders Magazine,* August 1988. Reproduced with permission of Marketmedia Group Co.

Mutual Building: The author.

Belcher's: *Richmond Times-Dispatch*, June 1988. Reproduced with permission.

Bull & Bear Club: *Richmond Times-Dispatch*, 2015. Reproduced with permission.

Fidelity Bank Building: *Richmond Times-Dispatch*, November 1980. Reproduced with permission.

Lawyers Title 1991 annual report: The author.

First National Bank Building: Photo by Scott Elmquist, *Style Weekly,* December 8, 2012. Reproduced with permission.

September 11, 2001, financial analysts lunch invitation: Courtesy of Louis O. Bowman, Jr.

Gayner, Buffett, Munger: Drawing by Christophe Vorlet. Reproduced with permission of the artist.

Anderson: *Richmond Times-Dispatch*, October 9, 1982. Reproduced with permission.

Ninth and Main looking south: Wikimedia Commons, 2015.

Mills' record: Courtesy of Charlie Mills.

Anderson & Strudwick plaque: Courtesy of David Ellington.

Epperson research: Courtesy of Jerry Epperson.

Merrill Lynch office sign: Photo courtesy of George Baskerville; reproduced with permission of the *Richmond Times-Dispatch.*

O'Malley's: *Richmond Times-Dispatch*, December 29, 1982. Reproduced with permission.

Former State–Planters Bank Building: The author.

Clyde Pitchford buttons: Courtesy of Sam E. Smith, Jr.

Richmond Stock Exchange: Courtesy of Virginia Historical Society.

Wheat First bullpen: *Richmond Times-Dispatch*, May 6, 1987. Reproduced with permission.

Scott & Stringfellow sign: Courtesy of Holiday Signs.

Wall Street Deli: The author.

Index

ph: photo sections

ABOUT THE AUTHOR

John B. Keefe., Sr., worked on and around Main Street for thirty-four years as a stockbroker, equity analyst, investment banker, and head of mergers and acquisitions for a public company. His career spanned bull markets and crashes, Dow 800 to Dow 17,000, Carter to Obama. He worked with many of *Main Street's* storytellers. John graduated from Washington and Lee University and holds the Chartered Financial Analyst® designation. He is married to Theresa Keefe and has two sons, Robert and John.